Carlitosics

By
Carlos Benjamin Torreblanca
aka
"Carlitos"

All Content Copyright.
© 2012, 2013 Carlos Benjamin Torreblanca
All Rights Reserved.
ISBN-10: 0985467304
ISBN-13: 978-0-9854673-0-2
Version 1.5

To all who desire something more,

    We are bound by seemingly inescapable human conditions. As a result, there are challenges restricting us from transcending beyond our current lived experience. This book approaches those challenges with the belief that every human can reach new levels of humanization by journeying into themselves and coming to terms with a greater picture of personal truth. Then codifying the self-knowledge they have gained, within a custom-tailored explanatory system, to be applied in the context of themselves.

    I am writing this book as humanity's self-appointed domestique. Jumpstarting people's metacognition by shedding light on the governing principles encountered on my way to becoming my realized self. Such universal truths transcend prepackaged, ready-made answers and are capable of liberating all to live a more humanistic, fulfilled life that can be shared with the world.

Contents

- Preface..iii
- 1 : Why..1
  - 1.1 : Vision..5
  - 1.2 : Goal..9
  - 1.3 : Journey..11
  - 1.4 : Inspiration..13
- 2 : Awareness...15
  - 2.1 : Identity..17
  - 2.2 : Purpose...21
  - 2.3 : Simplification..25
    - 2.3.1 : Living..29
- 3 : Letting Go..35
  - 3.1 : Idealism..39
  - 3.2 : Expectations..41
  - 3.3 : False Proxies...43
  - 3.4 : Self-Documentation...47
- 4 : Universal Truths..51
  - 4.1 : Reality...53
  - 4.2 : Nature..57
    - 4.2.1 : Duality...61
  - 4.3 : Ego...63
  - 4.4 : Fears...67
    - 4.4.1 : Testing...71
      - 4.4.1.1 : Equalizers..79
    - 4.4.2 : Perspective...83
  - 4.5 : Futility..91
    - 4.5.1 : Privilege..101
  - 4.6 : Freewill...113
  - 4.7 : Love...117
  - 4.8 : Life...119
- 5 : Human Systems..121
  - 5.1 : Problem Solving..127
    - 5.1.1 : Focus..133
      - 5.1.1.1 : Mindset...137
    - 5.1.2 : Control Method...139
- 6: Transcendence...145
  - 6.1 : Maintaining Solidarity..149

6.1.1 : Balance	153
6.2 : Your Beginning	157
Epilogue	159
Pedagogy	173

Preface

May I help you with those blinders? Exploiting through every vicissitude, modern day self-help gurus sell what they claim as a means to attempt to achieve it. The ol' "do as I say not as I do" methodology. Right off the bat this should raise a red flag hinting that their "alternative", blanket philosophies can only exist for them. Between the cracks of mass society. Not on the even playing field where it's necessary to reinstate overall balance for all to share a humanized existence.

    The definition of hypocrisy is personified by liars who can't even live up to standards they claim to embody. What they are is all they are. Pathetic, unqualified imposters fighting for the lead role in *A Jesus for Our Time*. Only seeking to establish mercenary relationships, while subjecting the virtue bound and other sentient forms of life to walk a path they simply cannot. If all are incapable of living by the merciless code these freakish divas preach—unassisted by hidden support—then gullible pilgrims are headed for wannabe Mecca. Groupies who decide this reality suffices continue existing in the shadows of weakness and compromise. Acting as demolishing parasites to the efforts of those who keep the world going through an honest day's work. Hoping, through action, for a better tomorrow.

Self-proclaimed, new age fakes are nothing more than pre-existing knowledge aggregators; clandestinely scouting the next photo op. Less concerned with their own journey than with that profitable gimmick they can rush off to a reverse engineering sweatshop, package with an all-encompassing legal disclaimer, and sell you. These one-trick ponies are bush-league in every respect. Except when it comes to targeting those in desperate need of hope. With the goal of converting them into instant disciples to keep their bullshit propaganda campaign on the fast track. In the end, it's all about them and you'll find this out after they get what they came for: to cop a feel on your wallet and add you to their customer base. Don't become a fashion victim of the latest human potential pyramid schemes. Consisting of ideologies with their own particular hang-ups. If a "leader's" moral compass isn't identical to yours (I seriously doubt it and this makes me confident you won't buy into their bullshit) there is no way they can tell you where you will find yourself. Hence, senseless discussions where they speak out of both sides of their mouths are a waste of time, no matter how convincing, because intellect can always justify. Maybe some are entertained by their psychobabble bullshit, but I find them masturbatorically assholish. These frauds know all the right monikers to make it seem like they know what they are talking about, but the delta between what they know and what they claim to know is a distance so large it can't be measured in light years. Another rack of moral-less criminals unworthy of honorable mention. Just curious, is it these clowns who are giving you your G2? If so, how's that working out for ya?

What did their hands really touch? Jerk-off things like email. They've probably never even done a single day of selfless backbreaking work. To them "work" is pulling rank with empty credentials while backstabbing to no end. Then putting their sin-stained fingerprints on the efforts of others. Also, who paved their way? We're these duncical empty suits generically stamped out by-products resulting from rising tide economic growth? Have they paid all their dues? Or have the people that they've leveraged just died off and that is why these egos have decided it's okay to run scot-free? Tell me cause I want to know. Where does their undeserved hubris come from—legacy? If they were privileged and their supposedly "solid" foundation was built upon the backs of others' sacrifices (meaning they have received without earning) then their journey is not accessible to the common man and therefore means jack shit. Put it next to all the other over-marketed, ordain by mail junk and toss it. I don't give a fuck who certified them or how many prissy little plaques they have hanging in their corner office. The only thing that matters is what you and I approve of as a result of looking within and determining what we believe to be true.

Since you and I will be spending time together, let's get one thing straight. I don't give a shit what armchair junkies (critics, haters, morons) say about my colloquially wild rhetoric because I don't write for them. They can go fuck themselves and stick to reading PG-13 crap—if even literate—that bears no relation to what life is actually about. See, I made it. I soloed the summit that is "I" with no Sherpas, no ropes, and no supplemental advantage. As truth is their kryptonite, I'm their worst nightmare. Their antithesis—persona non grata número uno! Allergic to bullshit, I let it be known. My work serves the struggling, underprivileged, realistic underdog. Not sheltered, never faced real shit assholes who perpetuate an existence by lying to the virtuous. Not to say you can't learn from my work if you are that asshole. Fortunately there is always time to land on the firm ground of reality before you are accepted into the most non-exclusive club in the world. It's called "Real Life Struggles". Also known as "normal" for ninety-nine percent of humanity. Membership isn't particular, but remember; only you can let yourself in.

For the record, I was not intellectually, monetarily, or egotistically obligated to share my journey and that's why my words maintain an air of integrity. I can back up what I write. I don't have to say what I'm going to do, cause I've already made my bones. I lived one painful word at a time in order to complete this monument on my own mental and monetary dime. Just so you know, the opportunity cost of writing this book was well over a million dollars and worth every penny. Self-actualization is priceless and without substitute. I have paid my fucking dues within a harsh reality I maintain to this day. Doing so has made me the person I can live with. I sleep well, harbor no regrets, and docent a crystal clear conscious. My credibility is rock-solid because moi's experiences link together without gaps commonly present in those whose learning curves are peppered with advantageous shortcuts. My qualifications include pain, suffering, and moving forward no matter what. I'm in the business of learning things the hard way aka the honest way. This means my choices are accessible to anyone who cares to make similar sacrifices in their own life, if they dare. You down?

Humanity's limitations are a result of how individuals direct their intellect. Culturally we're not incented to transcend our human conditions. Instead, we're encouraged to remain in a socially reinforced state of purgatory. A cult fueled by misled idealism in order to support the backbone of a materialistically bastardizing, capitalistic society. A prison style collective where false pretenses and sodomized ideals thrive. One where people imbue their bodies and minds with negative influences. And then claim to transcend by pumping distorted ideologies into products and services for you to buy. Like our culture needs another retarded piece of crap. I caution you all not to ogle fool's gold, being sold by modern snake oil salesmen, personifying past potholes of naïve American belief. Such as the American Dream. As soon as these heartless parasites smell "opportunity" they come out of the cuts like loked out locusts in a twit. Ready to sink barbed fangs resembling irremovable quills. More than happy to skip the pan and go straight into the fire when stalking the "almighty" dollar. Claiming to walk a line of integrity, but the fact they have to advertize credibility is proof they've already sold out. I never have and I never will.

Modern marketing is the greatest lie-producing engine in the history of the world. Only continuing to extend its reach because we fill this death machine's gas tank with the purchasing power of our hard-earned dollars. If companies' products are so damn great why don't they just keep them all? One has to wonder how we managed to survive a turbulent evolutionary history before the massive product explosion of the last century. Granted a few material items improve life, but do we really need so many external attachments? Besides, if products being forced upon us are infected with the same hypocrisy proprietors are struggling to conceal, how does any of this make sense? Oh wait, it doesn't.

Socio-cultural ethics have mutated into a steroid infused rape to squeeze the last fucking dollar out of everything. Regardless of negative implications that affect nature, life, and the rest of the connected universe. Advertisers are enjoying the role of slavemaster at the helm of this new form of indentured servitude coined "commercialism". Being perfect slaves, we pay to be marketed to. Then buy appealing, but ultimately unnecessary shit. And in turn—sometimes most whorishly—advertise these awareness anchors in ways that fill sin-lined coffers while unknowingly drowning our souls. Encouraging this evil cycle of materialism does nothing more than separate. We become obsessed with building an idealized identity. Endlessly draining our pocket books, while remaining internally unsatisfied. As a result, anything that resembles authenticity or originality is instantly devoured by our meaning starved culture whose appetite hungers for organic and natural, not artificial fulfillment. The not so apparent casualties? For every falsely persuaded believer of prepackaged lies, a million dreams are discarded. For every worshiped false prophet, a thousand real heroes remain unsung. Unfortunately this all too common tragedy happens repeatedly—swept under the carpet—in a culture overly preoccupied with self.

    This book is nothing more than a compilation of truths revealed to an unbridled heart that never gave up trying to discover itself amongst the disintegration of the American Ideal. A romanticized fairytale to which the term "well-adjusted" has lost all meaning. This anomaly's crumbling—according to fact not legend—is due in large part to the exposing of its cornerstone, fraudulent "masks". I have no respect for these so called "heroes" who are all about getting us to join the star culture bandwagon with the direct intention of increasing their Hollywood factor. All these attention whores are doing is expressing the manifestations of their ego, then creatively disguising shallow actions as worthy of respect. This is why they get none of mine. Still, just because I exercise and encourage reverse celebrity worship doesn't let me off the hook. No one gets off that easy unless jerking themselves off.

    I accept that it is my responsibility to provide an alternative to the bullshit, not just shit talk and criticize. Remaining stagnant and doing nothing to help solve the world's problems makes me no better. Besides, we already have enough folks doing that job just fine. I am not here to sell you another hoop dream. I'm here to deliver value that will work if you work. The point of writing this book was not to sell copies. If it sells so be it. If it doesn't, I don't give a fuck. Should people find my words valuable and one thing leads to another, great! I will feel eternally satisfied that I was able to help someone for the right reasons. I just want you to know that my first intention was to create outside of a self-serving, profit maximization attitude.

Preface

This book is a result of my real journey, where I was looking past all commercial and social propaganda to be able to connect with myself without someone telling me how to or selling me useless garbage along the way. This work is the highest example of what it claims—what's preached is practiced. It's not the result of targeted market research. Nor was it completed through leveraging resources such as ghostwriters, coffee go-getters or any other wannabes that modern publishing has enslaved as its little whores. Oh I'm sorry. Let me be politically correct: "special resources". I embody complete and utter disdain for those who claim to make the world a better place under the ruse of money. And yes, I shoot messengers. They are just concerned with receiving a steady. I am not. In the business of hope there can be no substitute for ultimate and absolute sincerity. Death to all exceptions.

I wrote this book because I felt I needed to say something that was missing. Something that I wish existed when I was struggling to find myself. Something that the majority of us have all forgotten. Had I not accepted this challenge it would've been the greatest mistake of my life. I wouldn't have been able to continue living and referring to myself as a "man". For the biggest sin is the sin of disbelief. Disbelief in oneself. It's unforgiveable not to share our gifts with the world. I did what I had to and I hope you'll do the same.

This book is the result of something that is real in all of us, but for many goes unnoticed because its possibility is never tapped into. Everyone embodies a uniqueness particular to them alone, but unless they decide to look within; gifts will lay buried under layers of unconquered fear and uncertainty. If your life's journey is about you then how could it make any sense to look elsewhere? This book represents my voyage to find myself and bridge my reality to an honest living by creating something meaningful. Something of value, which contributes by directly impacting the quality of each individual life it touches. Your experience with my labor is the tell-all of whether I have accomplished my goal or failed. The proof is in the pudding. You decide.

My intention was to get to the core of myself and make my own discoveries about what was true to me. What a different world this would be if everyone did that. Instead society's new normal is a morally bankrupt compromise where everyone is expected to meet somewhere in the middle. Fuck that! I say follow what you believe to be true, outside of external justification. If you don't agree with my findings, yet have your own self-formulated opinions, great! Please, share through hypocrisy free culminations. I just want people to think for themselves. Outside corrupt and misleading contexts, which have become synonymous with modern life. Don't be a fucking follower of others. Follow yourself. Where did all the unsung heroes go? Let you in on a little secret. That's us.

So many are blessed with the gift of being able to comprehend the bigger picture, yet consciously decide to fall short of transcending their human conditions. I can't tell you how many people I've known with more talent in their pinky finger than I have in my entire being for which this is the case. They just didn't act. Instead they became consciously fixated on parody waste, which in itself is a type of purgatory. I'm referring to the point of awareness where people arrive at truth and instead of moving forward remain at the level of rules, safety, casual conversation, standards, ethical debate, galactic compromise, religious affiliation, over-the-top payback, ruthless pillaging, support groups, rule bending, dream circumcision, loneliness induced appeasement, mind-numbing specifications, carnal desires, satirical entertainment, neglect, flattery, frustration, shit talking, fake excuses, denial, pathetically incremental pay grades, sarcastic witticisms, creatively disguised social commentary, sinister acts, indecent imitation, familial dysfunction, ridic racist undertones, disguised loyalty, money, Pollyanna social change, speculation, fame, terrorism, threats, prestige, wealth accumulation, pompousness, dull social miming, unhealthy addiction, undeserved indulgence, anal maintenance, divaesque drama, memorable mention, unwarranted conformity, reflection, fascination, curiosity, monkeywrench sabotage, protest, bourgeois slavery, keeping up with the "Whatevers", rebellion, moral abstinence, complaining, preference, venting, emotions, opinions, fashion, doomed politics, the latest trend, the next best thing, zero gravity ethics, chemically induced states, endless unaccepted propositions, disgusting humor, euphemisms, dysphemisms, compartmentalized Zen, vernacular, mockery, working the system, intellectual posturing, dishing humiliation, perpetual mourning, rehab, ridicule, observations, one too many false starts, disturbing perfection, acts of misogyny, supporting the untested, civil disobedience, cruelty, methods, styles, cell-born radicalism, artistic representation, securing unconformable salvation, violence, cultural identity, playing the victim, tacky nitpicking, wasteful indecision, comfortable ignorance, slimy gossip, beat to death strategy and many other facets circling but; avoiding direct action aimed at what is absolutely necessary. The list goes on forever, which is why I won't. I think you get the picture. The onus is on you.

It's easy to point out the bad and then live buffered through layers of separation. Anyone can do that and most people do. I challenge you with providing an alternative solution based on your firsthand interpretation. Approach what disrupts the world by first confronting what disturbs you. It's hard, isn't it? Well, if all you can do is point out the obvious instead of contributing something of value where does that leave you? Are you going to give up without a fight and stay tied to the problem or act and become an integral part of the solution? Time is a factor since we don't live forever. Your lack of immediacy should make you question your priorities and whether or not what you claim to represent falls into a secondary, less important category disguised as nepotism. Be honest, does it?

It's tempting to preach auspiciousness up every step of the self-actualization ladder, but such behavior is counter-productive. As is falling into the trap of placating those with an "Are you there yet?" mentality. The goal is to get to the top of your mountain so you can translate the ultimate view to humanity through your unique contribution. This is why it is necessary for people to develop a keen second-level awareness in order to consciously drive their awakened sensations past roadblocks by exercising the real forgotten lost arts: freewill and direct action. We must teach ourselves techniques suited to evaluate current behaviors and their compliance or lack of accord with what is at hand. In other words, make shit happen instead of just talking or thinking about change like every other poser.

Looking to the world to tell you what you should or shouldn't do is a dangerous proposition, because socially engrained ideals fuel impressions. One hope is that if we follow the status quo presented by these depictions we will be directed toward our ideal path. Unfortunately with no confirmable single entity guiding the collective unconscious it makes more sense to look within for direction. You are responsible for you? What a revolutionary idea! The question you should be asking yourself is "What am I going to do about it?" How 'bout turning your dilemma into a solution? Just a thought. The day we stop responding to this question with direct action is the day we die. And just so you don't confuse the concept of death allow me to clarify. Most people completely misunderstand mortality. We don't die when our body ceases to function. We die when we no longer harbor the will to seek out possibilities associated with personal growth. This is the real value of every human to society. Man's heart beats louder than any drum. Find your beat and move to its rhythm. It's that simple.

Preface

Hope exists in setting off on an individual journey to the deepest recesses of our soul to uncover what holds us back from transcending. As always, looking outside to understand what's within is futile. Doing so we remain stuck with the option of being satiated by the incomplete, ethereal theories and methods of others: those never entirely suited to us. Leave everything behind that is not essential to your existence and say your own words. Although you may receive guidance along your path the golden rule is to always look to yourself as the ultimate deciding factor. This is absolutely critical because the connections you establish will be unidentifiable by others—no matter what they claim—because they do not have the access of experiencing life from your unique, irreplicable perspective. Only you know what it's like to be you. Good luck and I'll see you on the other side!

Still learning and burning…

Carlitos Tonelluro

1 : Why

It all began with a spark! I wanted change. Therefore, I had to. My ignition was kicked-off by the realization that if I continued to live "by numbers" the awareness pitfalls of canonical, check-the-box thinking were soon to become my final resting place. Although at first glance I may come off as picaresque, that's hardly the case. This is what men who've been weaned on harsh reality sound like. After doing everything "right" I remained land-locked in a never-ending societal scrum. My journey revealed itself as a quest for personal truth. To in return share with humanity a unique contribution through knowledge gained. I came to the crossroads in my life and was faced with a very difficult decision — risk losing everything I had worked for — that couldn't be undone. The only respectable option was to take my body and mind to hell and see if I could make it back from self-imposed exile and crucifixion. I committed social and career suicide and lived to tell. In madness I found method. Awareness itself became my creative process. Eventually I reached a state of social pariah where I no longer respected my fears, ditched my hero worship, and decided to leave everything familiar behind in an attempt to say my own words. "Who am I to myself?" I wanted to be my own anti-hero.

My work serves not as your explanatory system, but as an exploratory reference of what was left of me when I arrived at myself. My journey was about getting to where I could really begin to live in accordance with my beliefs. Believing firmly in the doctrine of freewill, this became the singular focus of my life. My conscious kept dragging me back to the fact that I was not living up to my potential. As a result, transparent moments of happiness did not satisfy my recurring yearnings. So in an attempt to rediscover myself, I didn't just leave the farm behind. I burned it to the ground.

My quest for the absolute has led me beyond what I thought possible and further than I would've wanted to go had I known what lay ahead. So why is any journey important? Because, the journey is all about confronting your fears. The journey is the story and the story can only be original if you decide to abandon preset destinations fueled by infantile infatuations. Why go through the trouble to revolutionize yourself when you have been germinated in an alternate modality? That answer always has to come from you. You are the one who needs to believe in the plot you are crafting. The sacrifices required for such an isolated endeavor are inconceivable. However, you must remember. Whether alone or not, you have to be able to do things by yourself. If you can't run alone then be prepared to suffer at the mercy of the herd.

How do we begin? We think as lone wolves. Independently assessing our internal inventory of realness. This is directly tied to a distancing from our false surroundings. Distance allows us to remain objective. Outside the infected spheres of influence governed by society's collective conscious. This will grant you the space needed to determine the standards by which you will live. You must learn to trust this void because it will provide the necessary environment to train your mind to determine independently. If we don't set our own mark, and enforce it, there are consequences because

1 : Why

we live up to the standards we set for ourselves or lack thereof. Man is not an island, but in this world of bullshit it serves his higher purpose if he can be one when he needs to be.

We can only access internal powers that govern if we stop bitching and complaining and begin to search for the hidden entities, laws, and truths that regulate our lives. To find ourselves we must leave empty ambitions behind and begin to trust ourselves to the point of demonstrating extraordinary sincerity and competence for the gauntlet we'll have to take up. This battle is the most difficult fight of our lives. It begins with an unfledgling commitment to see things through to the end. By signing on the dotted line with our blood, sweat, and tears.

1.1 : Vision

Detrimental factors leading to the current state of humanity have stretched and torn society's cultural fabric. The social mending necessary to reconnect us with a humanistic path requires that each harness cosmic powers within. We all have a responsibility to assist in the transcendence of mankind because we are only here on the backs of past generations. Propped up by massive, monumental sacrifices. Positively contributing to society's cultural fabric, and in the process moving the world in an increasingly humanizing direction, is something we are all capable of if we so choose.

    My dream is not my own, it is everyone else's: help restore the inner peace of humanity by restoring myself. By solving our own problems, indirectly we solve the world's. For we are one in the same. Twin parallels of infinite relatability. Joined by an invisible umbilical cord connecting all life. The better we understand ourselves the better we understand others. Knowledge of oneself can have far-reaching effects in the context of a contribution to society. By learning the inner workings of our psychosis we find new ways to relate. Humans, although different in many respects, share deeply engrained qualities. Due to the fact that our existence is firmly rooted in nature. Reconnected with deeper, more basic aspects of ourselves we become active change agents aligned with the greater causes of this world.

Encouraging people to become their own heroes unleashes real value upon society. As people develop strong tendencies within their areas of confidence (whatever they maybe) and are encouraged to do so, they become confident explorers of their uniqueness. Pondering how self-discovered treasures may be crafted into a gift that will humanize. Eventually contributing to the overall good. Areas of confidence are one's starting point. Something a person feels proficient in doing from which similarities of knowledge can be established and applied toward additional avenues of self-discovery. A unique contribution begins to synergize when individuals are able to reconnect with themselves at a multitude of awareness levels, and understand not only their nature, but also the natural elements encompassing human existence. These deeper connections facilitate thinking which makes it possible to understand how one can live to realize greater humanization through the power of choice. Whatever their driving motivations, people must follow their hearts in order to create a unique contribution worthy of being labeled "innovation". To the extent that they learn how to innovate innovation for themselves, it is my belief that the world will change. Slowly, but surely.

In each individual there sleeps an original dreaming of being awakened. This original is equipped with inner gifts capable of saving humanity through individually rising to new levels of potential. People are best convinced by what they discover. It is my goal to facilitate those discoveries that inspire in hopes of igniting people's journey by awakening their deeper senses.

Individuals are so unique that one-size-fits-all philosophies never come close to satisfying internal questions like the depth generated understanding that one

1.1 : Vision

can experience when they decide to become the focus of their journey. We all have a chance to interpret life and create an explanatory system built to suit ourselves and share the benefits of our self-discovery with the world. To each his own destiny. One for all is all for one.

1.2 : Goal

My goal for this book was to create a contextual architecture in which people could explore themselves and facilitate their own discoveries. I want to help you get to the core of yourself to actualize your hidden potentialities. My unofficial motto? First, live by example. Then share. You are under the tutelage of yourself, but at least you have my real example.

I have sought out, and will continue to do so until my death, a colorful life of firsts (first experiences). These adventures have provided the circumstances amongst which I have been able to discover myself in raw, unexplored newness. I am not in this for the money. I am here to test myself hard and push limits to deliver value capable of humanizing the world. Having traveled the agonizing chaos and misery of self-struggle that accompanies these barnburners, I want to share what I have learned to enable people to transcend their specific human conditions. I believe this can be achieved if people learn how to live in accordance with the universal truths and natural laws that are revealed to them when they look within.

Cultivating this deeper relationship with yourself is not about imposing your ego to force becoming who you are not. On the contrary, it's about understanding how to embrace and support yourself in a way which leads you to becoming the person you are in your heart. Just like no one can "out-Carlitos" me. No one can be a better you than yourself. Decide to get to know this you by discovering yourself.

1.3 : Journey

The journey will enlighten to the extent that one is willing to sacrifice for what is desired. It's not about justifying based on theoretical calculation. It's about living things out. A single moment at a time. Not everything can be intellectualized and that is why journeys are necessary. If we don't go, we won't know. If we knew life would be a destination. That is not the case. By borrowing from the learning curves of others you will never reap the full benefit of their exploration. Many people borrow so excessively that even when they accomplish, they don't deserve credit or applause. This discrepancy is easily observed when one looks beyond expired credentials or recent results, straight to the wisdom (or lack thereof) that a person actually wields.

We find meaning in the process of working for it ourselves. Your journey is the learning curve through which you will find yourself and get to a place where you can begin to live as you choose. Brace yourself for change because we only discover at the edge of our limits. Not on comfortable, familiar ground. If things are too tolerable, diluted is the impetus to move beyond.

The journey is not about starting with an end in mind unless all you want is a predictable path to something already within your realm of reason. You will not be able to figure everything out before moving forward. Your journey will only be original if you decide to leave all maps behind and follow inclinations deep within your soul. This means ditching familiar landmarks that have guided you. There are no safety nets allowed on this trip. It's okay to not know where you are going so long as you understand why you are traveling.

Following your internal compass will bring you to the home in your heart and your responsibility is to hold onto whatever is there and never let go. Your deep conscious is inviting you to explore what restores its inner peace. Search for your absolute and refrain from objectives and ideals. Instead let questions guide you to the actions you must take to answer them. As always, there are no dumb questions just bad answers. Identify intuitions that arise from observing the multitude of semantic connections in your mind. Follow your instincts by going with the largest associations you see and don't second-guess yourself. Go with your gut!

Everything in the context of lived experience exists along a continuum that begins at birth and ends with death. There are no markers along a true journey. The only marker is you and where you currently stand. There are no successes or failures. Only indicators as to what are the adjustments necessary to progress along your chosen path. The choice to incorporate change or remain stagnate ultimately lies within your hands. You won't always be able to dictate the pace of self-discovery. Sometimes you will have to run. Other times you will need to walk. But mark my words. You will always have to move forward, no matter what.

1.4 : Inspiration

Inspiration is the only true revolution. Beyond the rejuvenating effects we experience from sharing in others purest hopes our journey is about following internally guided captivations, we are magnetically drawn to. It is your responsibility to personally define the path through which possibilities may be explored to unveil your distinctive gift upon the world.

Pre-existing knowledge is a double-edged sword with a dangerously sharp tip. When we observe (and admire) a trail that has been blazed by another we must avoid the temptation to follow the same pre-carved route if attempting to cultivate a unique contribution. Instead let us honor pre-existing contributions as important reminders that others have singlehandedly defined their own paths with the intention of giving back something personal and realize we need to do the same. Otherwise the concept of living through comparison will enter the picture. Living through comparison is not living. It's comparing.

2 : Awareness

Awareness is consciously bringing the subconscious—everything from the infinitesimally small to the infinitely large—into our ever-expanding mental universe. Contrary to popular opinion, awareness is not an achieved state of suspended animation for which a box can be checked once attained. It's an allusive, fluctuating target that requires continuous adjustment to be accurately perceived. As we become increasingly aware new areas of our subconscious, that were previously undecipherable, begin to take observable shape. Our awareness expands to the extent that we are able to classify its current state and explore what lies unassimilated in the peripheral of our conscious.

We are responsible for identifying areas of our lives that we must realistically come to terms with, in order to move on and live life as we see fit. There isn't much wiggle room here. To transcend what is keeping you from actualizing your realized self you must become aware, not only of where you stand and the state of your existence; but of your ability to see past distractions. Straight to the core of your essence. Often times it's not things that change, but the way we perceive them. Therefore, in order to trust our ability to change we must have faith in our ability to see.

Life is lived in the awareness we provide for ourselves. Awareness, in every sense of the word, allows us to experience connectedness to the extent that we are accurately interpreting and conscious of the present moment. As our observative patterns settle into a fluctuating, push-and-pull rhythm of expansion; it becomes natural to trust and follow sensations emanating from an awakened state. However, just because we remain aware does not immunize us from the influence of cerebral observations. It's coming to terms with findings that allows us to move on while still maintaining discoveries as integrated patches of our universal fabric.

When we are consciously conscious of our path and in direct alignment with our higher purpose, we become powerful change agents. Directing our future through the choices with which we decide each moment. You can really only understand yourself, your sensibilities, and the context of your entirety within the broader picture of what is your discovered self. Eventually with perspective everything becomes important and then nothing is.

2.1 : Identity

It is useful to know who you are by knowing who you are not. Then deciding to define yourself not by rationalization, but by action. Have you ever locked eyes with yourself in the mirror and asked, "Where's your heart at"? How about, "Who are you to yourself"? You should try it sometime. It can be quite revealing to gift yourself the opportunity to consciously reflect upon the details of how you associate your existence. Independent of all external contexts.

Understanding who we are has to do with locating clues to what we have consciously and subconsciously manifested. We manifest our lives with traces of that which our heart secretly harbors. It is through these disguised pathways that our soul attempts to provide clues that reunite us with what really matters and why we are here. Hazy or sometimes even in-your-face bright red flags hint at us to take particular notice of an area of our lives that is aching to be explored. If we refuse to explore these inherent possibilities for growth, then we accept full responsibility for limiting our own development.

The crisis of identity runs deep because people do things that stun their authenticity. It's a harsh pill to swallow realizing how different reality is from the false identities we often construct if fear driven. An even harsher reality to accept is that if we don't alter course the rest of our lives will be wasted trying to create a bridge to a lie that doesn't even exist. Scary isn't it? It is impossible for us to feel connected to something greater if the majority of our identity is constructed in false proxies. Far away from the home that is our heart.

The most common, misleading identity yardstick—so excessively overused in our current cultural landscape that it is going out of style—is association by title. Titles are nothing more than ego badges. Those whose strength of identity emanates from sporting them are not strong at all. Misguided at best. If you live through titles (bestowed by others or yourself) then you must pop this bubble of pretention surrounding your fake-ass existence. This is the only way to deflate a stratospheric ego so that it descends back into the atmosphere of reality and firmly lands humbly on ground zero.

As a society we have to let the false parts of ourselves die and quit trying to create compartmentalized identities, in constant state-of-newness labyrinths, where we in fact get lost. Once you accept who you are you will be able to move on and grow. It's not so much about choosing what to become, as it is about discovering how to connect with your deeper yearnings seeking reunion. This is accomplished by letting go of ideologies in order to allow our inner voice to ring true. Slowly, but surely; guiding us to ultimate destiny. A place we cannot reach through control or intellectualization because it requires that we go beyond who we are and what we know today to realize a new tomorrow.

People are not succession candidates. Every person is a special being within which a unique contribution is buried and waiting to be discovered. We have to look beyond the cloth from which we have been cut and further than the modalities that past experiences have

2.1 : Identity

germinated us in. Even though it may seem scary, if you break from normlessness you will not cease to exist. In fact, you will become more yourself than ever before.

As our journey continues, identity becomes an increasingly important reference point for researching ourselves and reflecting upon findings through daily living. Treasures can only be unearthed if we take the time to decipher our intuitions and act according to their truth. Let us farm our soul and patiently distill wisdom from the spirited moments of passion we experience, secretly hinting at our purpose. End the scavenger hunt for your identity by turning to what is inside, now.

2.2 : Purpose

Passion is purpose. Exploring our passions to their most profound depths can be helpful in guiding us to an oasis where we are nourished by a personal nirvana of purpose. What is it about what we love to do that reveals purpose? What convictions do we have locked in our subconscious, awaiting flight into the sky of possibilities? There's only one way to find out. All one has to do is listen to their heart and decode surfacing emotions. Distance is never suggested. The key is to be in tune with your emotional constitution. If ignored, emotions will just keep reminding till you wear to the point of breakdown or an unhealthy psychological state. Still, breakdowns are breakthroughs.

Humans are amazing creatures composed of highly advanced emotional circuitry. Emotions are the warning signals of needs. They are the informative messengers of life. Alerting us as to what needs to be addressed and with what level of urgency. When we are tired we need sleep. When we are hungry we need food. When we are horny we need sex. When we are lonely we need to socialize. Emotional fulfillment through activities, which satisfy necessities, is evidence of our highly developed response mechanisms that exist to increase our survivability. If we ignore their obviously painful presence in our feedback loops, manifestations of uncomfortable torment persist. Nothing we do to circumnavigate or placate them, in ways other than what they require, works. We all have a burden to bear. Emotions are the keen guides facilitating necessary mental and physical states to face such. They empower us with the ability to identify deeply rooted roadblocks, within our psychosis, that need to be confronted to put the past behind us for good.

Failing to classify our emotional chemistry is why we end up only partially satisfied with what we think we wanted after we obtain it. For this reason it is the responsibility of our discerning conscious to learn how to acquire knowledge capable of satisfying deeper, fundamental yearnings. Not just surface-level infatuations. Shelve the stoicism and enough with the acquiescence already! Let's not disguise this search by being like every other laissez-faire practitioner pretending to "go with the flow" regardless of whatever happens in life. Even if at an emotional level turmoil is present. Realize that in this moment this is you suppressing what needs to come to the surface and be dealt with.

We have to get down to business and ask ourselves, "What do I really want and why do I want it?" Now ask yourself, "How many bloody, sacrificial rounds with my fears am I prepared to go to get what I want out of my life?" If your answer is frivolous or anything less than "Whatever it takes!", you may want to do some soul searching to determine whether or not you are just another one of those people who is in lust with the idea of wanting something. The process of arriving at what we want can feel like a mini-quest of its own. This is not a time of contraction toward ideological pursuits we have logically manipulated ourselves to desire. In effect, backwards rationalizing what should never ever be tampered with. This is a time of expansion that demands scraping unsound, archetypal logic; solely commissioned to suit shortsighted, mainstream justification. Envision ways to incorporate newly discovered findings outside the logical scope of your mind, but within the emotional realm of your heart.

When you are stuck trying to decide what it is you want start walking open-mindedly down the path of possibilities, while donning a humble pair of shoes. Try things out. A lot of things. Invest in yourself. Give your all and see where things go. You may have to stumble over and over again to discover your gift. In fact, life requires failure as a prerequisite to finding out what it is we are good at. Through this absolutely necessary struggle we are tested and the best of ourselves must rise to the occasion. This is how we find out what we are made of! Only by being forced to survive will we discover what keeps us alive.

We are not looking for a string of victories, but threads of commonality that hint at the raw and organic flavor of our purpose. Gather enough experience to be able to cross-reference your past. Pinpointing your passions' humble, minimal beginnings. What it is about their origins, which if structured properly around goals will make you want to wake up every morning motivated to tackle life's challenges head-on? It can be useful to explore the universe that is you. Specifically your uniqueness. It all comes down to knowing what is the daily bread you require for proper nourishment. From there decide not to ignore findings. Embrace with a deadlock. Once you know what you are here to do don't get sidetracked by looking left or right into alleys of obscurity. Go straight toward that which illuminates your spirit.

Only you can wrestle the necessary fortitude to push yourself where you want to go. To make your purpose your reality you have to love what you do so much that you hate it. Yes, that much. This attitude will keep you going through the adversity you will have to endure to get there. The alternative is much worse. If you do not do what you are passionate about your life will become a never-ending chore. Devouring your spirit from the inside-out, as do terminal diseases. Hell, you might even get one because whatever was alive in you has revolted and eaten away at your insides. Because you never allowed energies to be used for a purpose other than internal affliction. People with no defined purpose (probably out of guilt for having not defined one) constantly have to keep justifying their existence. Otherwise in their minds they cease to exist. This illusion of existence is often defended through repeating the most spirit-starving, meaningless exercises known to man. Pretty fucking sad.

Do you want to feel the scarring burn from self-inflicted ropes of oppression castrating your spirit's life generating limbs? Or do you want permanent liberation, through the action of your own hands, so you can feel like a bird released? Tend the flame that is your passion and you will feel the warmth of hope igniting your energies to speed you along the way. All the way to what is the greatest home man can ever know. Purpose. Tell me. Which is the mountain you will mine for the rest of your life? It's your call.

2.3 : Simplification

Maturing and hopefully growing wiser through accumulated experience, one would think that our lives become increasingly simple. So why is the complete opposite phenomena so prevalent? Are poor choices to blame? How about unexercised freewill? One thing's for certain. Our culture is in desperate need of lifestyle reduction surgery. By simplifying our lives we greatly improve the quality of our lived experience. True bliss resides in the protective shadow of simplicity, beneath a cloak of anonymity. A place the impulsive novice tends to shy away from. Strictly due to an inability to surrender the unnecessary. Instead of letting natural juices flow in a trusting manner.

It's easy to complicate our lives, yet incredibly difficult to simplify them once they become overloaded with nonsensical bullshit. Our ability to problem solve becomes encroached when we're dealing with too much. Why not make it easier to solve the puzzle that is us by clearing the path to ourselves, for ourselves. The concept is easy enough, but building a life on such a pretext requires conscious commitment and a ton of hard work. The simplification I refer to deals not only with the material world we physically interact in, but also the psychological landscape we navigate daily.

Is more really necessary? It seems to me the governing principle in the world is: the less you have, the less you need. I believe we only need what we think we need and even that can be too much. Has it ever occurred to you that the frills and fanfare of a first world, modern life are just self-embraced distractions without any purpose? Shielding us from exactly what it is we need to confront. You can try getting wherever you are going with more, but it's going to be harder and maybe even impossible. Do you really want to be held responsible for taking all your physical and psychological baggage everywhere you go? When you die you take nothing. Not even your body. Ashes to ashes, dust to dust baby.

Insatiability and looking for happiness in the wrong places seem to be common drivers leading people to desire more. Regardless of their socioeconomic status. If my generalized conclusion strikes a nerve ask yourself, "What am I compensating for by filling my life with all this crap?" There is absolutely no point in creating a smokescreen between you and your reality because it only blinds you. If you continue to do this you will always view the world from an inaccurately skewed perspective. Further alienating your ability to see what is really going on.

Existing with less shows you are made of more. People who don't understand this are far too busy blindly compensating for their fears in the wrong ways. Less is more because everything we surround ourselves with creates the expectation and demands of a relationship with it. Whether we acknowledge trappings or not. Since complexity is the enemy of freedom that which drifts in the peripheral areas of life (without a place in the grand scheme of things) will eventually become burdening, cumbersome, distractive, and ultimately detrimental to growth. Just decide whether you would rather entertain a relationship with a complex, buffered lie. Or a simple, but basic reality.

2.3 : Simplification

It is essential to understand that which we do not use, in every sense, but store is also detrimental to our development. Any amount of energy devoted away from our higher purpose is wasted unless such investment is absolutely necessary for survival. Only then is maintaining something as part of your universal fabric justified. Return to a simpler existence by implementing a reward system that is geared at recognizing actions that reconnect you with only what is necessary. Establish peace with that reality. Your reward? To be fulfilling your life's purpose and building a meaningful existence in the process. It is egotistical and wasteful to do with more what can be done with less.

2.3.1 : Living

Control your position in life by living in the black, not the red. Purse strings and all. Black implies living within your means throughout every fiber of your universal fabric. Respecting healthy boundaries whose purpose is to provide adequate territory for you to develop the prerequisite, foundational footing necessary for complete autonomy. Such is what designates adulthood. Regardless of age. Red living implies that your universal fabric has not been fortified to qualify for the next stage of your journey. You have to earn your way by paying as you go. No exceptions. If you proceed without stepping up to the plate and addressing this delta, it will tip the overall balance of your lived experience toward unwanted chaos. It's questionable whether living in the red can even be termed "living" because of the turbulence it subjects unhealthy risk takers to. Just like revving an engine into a dangerously high rpm range, eventually something is bound to give. It always does. Just a matter of time.

Were we to construct a hypothetical balance sheet, where all components of your universal fabric were evaluated against a marker of honesty, we would be able to determine what you actually earned and can sustainably maintain as a result of how your path has been paved. I cannot emphasize enough, there are no easy steps on the treacherous road to self-actualization. This cobblestone path is paved with integrity by your hard-earned experience. If you bite off more than you can chew and then get cornered into a difficult situation, who's fault is it that you are stuck? Realize that others' purpose is not to act as your crutch. Constantly bailing you out of poor life choices. The sooner you do, the quicker the level and quality of your responsibility will begin to develop as a precursor to doing big things on your own.

Besides, what's the point of overextending our greedy reach just to end up living in the danger zone? It's stressful and can be very taxing on our mind, our body, and therefore handicap the expression of our soul's higher purpose. We live in an incorrigible culture that preaches it's acceptable to enjoy before we deserve. And by pushing boundaries we shouldn't. This undermines how our association of value is formed, because by not earning honestly we don't respect. Value is incomprehensible to those who don't earn justly. They have no idea what it takes to do so. They can assume, but that is a far cry from knowing and unfortunately it is their loss.

The concept of red versus black living applies not only to monetary expenditures, but to any other area of life where what is received is not commensurate to effort. Operating in the red causes us to accrue all types of debt: psychological, emotional, physical, monetary, energetic, etcetera. As a result, our developmental tab reflects a negative foundational balance we must at some point payoff. In my opinion the sooner the better. Aren't you tired of owing? Decide to pay life forward, invest in your future, and reap the benefits of wisdom by living in the black. You owe it to yourself.

Determining whether one is living in the red is calculated on a case-by-case basis. Through in-depth self-diagnosis. Gauging relevant factors accurately requires

2.3.1 : Living

a sensitivity unique to the operator's perspective. Hard to miss clues become evident when one is barely "cutting it" and showing signs of stress, which inevitably leads to breakdown. On the other hand, if a person is thriving. Continuing to test themselves more and more and becoming stronger. I'd say they are on the right track. Maybe they could even push themselves a bit further. If one is always successful tests aren't hard enough. Consistent, regular success indicates this because we don't pass all tests. If we do, they are too damn easy. Passing with flying colors makes us think we are better than we really are. Especially when the runway is groomed by others for us to succeed. The oddity here is failure, not fortitude. Rank pulling closet champions whose goal is to maintain a perfect record by riding coattails or avoiding real challenge, circumventing situations where failure or loss is a likely possibility, are ignorantly living within the realm of their ego and its deceptive protection.

People do a great job robbing themselves of experiencing the benefits provided by a painfully constructed learning curve, when they sideline self-control at their ego's beckon. Living in the red causes one to act in ways their sensibilities never would, under black conditions. Directly impacted is sound judgment. Decision cycles in the red are not independent of external, negatively influential factors that must now be considered instead of avoided all together. This makes life difficult, as many more complexities must be juggled. Greatly hindering one's ability to make purpose-aligned, uncompromising choices. Don't be pushed into perversion by subjecting yourself to self-prescribed condemnation. You determine your dose of reality and you commit to taking it. If the mixture isn't right you know whom to blame.

What makes no damn sense is why so many people pressure themselves in counterproductive ways. Those running directly contrary to purpose. And no, such behavior cannot be attributed to external phenomena: i.e. Mercury in retrograde, full moons, barometric pressure fluctuations, or bad luck. Instead of taking risks where it counts: self-discovery, education, personal development goals, physical fitness, creating unique contributions, etcetera. They apply ass-backwards, kamikaze ego-logic to decisions regarding practical matters (finances, health, safety, etcetera) and subsequently maintain a psychology that only leads to negative repercussions. Ironically, positive risk makes one more proficient at solidifying and retaining a black position. All but guaranteeing increased future freedom. Red risks increase unwanted chaos by opening a Pandora's box of revolving door problems. Overstepping solid foundational steps and making egotistical, entitled decisions in the red leads to mistakes. Some of which we can never correct, but for which the complete responsibility of ownership falls on the culprits who have made them—us.

Just because our star culture figures out increasingly creative ways to gain access to things doesn't mean we've earned them or that we deserve them. Hell, even when we are able to afford things doesn't mean we've earned them. These are trademark overbuying behaviors colluding with our undeserving ego that will forever think it is entitled to more.

People leverage all types of shortcuts to obtain what they cannot on their own and therefore don't deserve. Credit, drugs (street and prescribed; for pleasure or performance), information that shouldn't be hoarded, relationships, privilege, thievery, opportunism disguised as service, exaggerated credentials, body mutation, etcetera. The list goes on and on and on. There are so many ways to cheat others and ourselves by chasing false ideals that lure our ego into short-term gains. Hidden are very severe long-term consequences. If we constantly reward ourselves for encouraging bad behaviors then we become irresponsible custodians to

2.3.1 : Living

our development. By doing so we compromise our ability to control our position and risk losing the freewill to command destiny. Belly up and helpless is where we find ourselves when we live in the red.

Living in the black is about why making sure our reward systems are geared toward helping us walk the straight and narrow. Maximizing our potential by steering us clear of negative triggers. It's not easy, but it's necessary. You must gradually learn how to walk the line between reward and discipline. Between harshness and finesse. Between pride and confidence. Between respect and worship. Between blame and forgiveness. The reality is we can only learn how to navigate this tightrope by cautiously walking it everyday.

Speaking of days, whatever happened to saving for a rainy one? When you test yourself you will be the rainmaker on purpose. A lot of good this does you if you are so bound by shitty, self-created circumstances that any positively life changing opportunities have to be put on layaway because you still haven't learned the fundamentals of what it is to be an independent and responsible adult. Moderation is key. You have to prep your life with a little leeway and a few stored resources to make changes as required. Maybe you tire of getting paid to pretend and tell your boss "You can take this job and shove it up your ass!" Or just decide you are tired of monotonous bullshit and break fresh ground on your own. My point? Have options. Always be thinking several plays ahead. Frequently peer down the road of possibilities. When you can work extra and are not tired, bang it out. Later when in need, you may not have what it takes at that moment in time and dip into your reserves for the right reasons. At all costs, never ever let your position be controlled by anything or anyone other than yourself.

Most head-cases live in a red hell for so long that by the time they want to change they are stuck in a catch-22 death funnel. No getting out of this black hole's mouth without anything short of a miracle or incredible determination. Here the gravitational pull of fate will have its way because calls from destiny were put on hold or ignored. Prior to this cries for help didn't really make sense, but for once they will. At this point there is almost nothing that can be done. Controls are set to autopilot. Terminal disaster is eminent. Those aboard are just along for the ride on a roller coaster of destruction. The only thing that might save them is a total-life reset. At a huge personal expense and I don't just mean money. I mean everything must change. Adjustments are out of the question. I'm talking cataclysmic revolution.

When someone gets to this point it means they don't know shit and it's time for them to shut their self-persuading mouths and listen. What they are doing is not working and never will. Otherwise they wouldn't resemble the self-afflicted, satanic puppet in this conundrum. They have to reach out beyond their ego's logic and become full-time students exploring with a humble step in their walk. Very few people will ever attempt this dangerous rescue because so many are ego bound to the point of avoiding reality at all costs. To these delusional folks a wasted life plagued by lies becomes justifiable. Regardless of what this selfish act does to them or others. Their only hope? A Hail Mary pass requiring very rough re-entry procedures into the atmosphere of reality. A last bid to risk losing everything in a non-guaranteed attempt to save what is real. Life is all about trade-offs my friend, and this is the biggest. Let me introduce you two.

"Hi! I'm Sacrifice. Pleasure to make your acquaintance!"

3 : Letting Go

Letting go is difficult, but instantly makes life so much easier. Presently, there are more awareness traps than in the entire history of man. Although indirectly (primarily through society's collective unconscious), these pitfalls keep us from uniting with deeper purpose. Whether it be deceptive product bundling disguised as "innovation integration", intended to address recently contrived needs we didn't even know we had, or societal norms in general. We must be aware of what we share our life with that ultimately blocks our path.

This involves sorting through our physical and psychological landscapes to identify and eliminate barriers preventing us from living the most of ourselves. Let go of what is holding you back and unnecessary. Let go of what is keeping you from opening up. Without space nothing can be created or explored because there is no room. You need space to figure yourself out in the mental domain just as in the physical realm where it is easier to work uncluttered.

In re-establishing a relationship with the core of ourselves we must remember, limitations are not from what we don't have; but from what we don't know. Knowledge is power, but never forget; action—destiny. Feel instant relief by letting go of what is no longer empowering and enriching because it has become another energy depleting responsibility with no place or purpose in the grand scheme of things. Rejoice in the act of discarding insignificance because holding on to it doesn't help you in the least. The truth about ownership: it's a myth. We don't own anything. We curate possessions and when we die, exit we do in humbling fashion. By disregarding paths that lead nowhere we will be able to travel further. Unencumbered by confusion and needless distraction.

When it comes to your psyche remove debris of judgment. Buff out tainted memories from rough past experiences. Unobstruct the lens through which you view the world, in order to use it to the best of its ability. Release yourself from the spirit-crushing grip of archaic collective standards. Reunite with the essentials of being human. Scrap useless nostalgia. Live for yourself and your time. Instead of mourning the disappearance of dogmatic traditions, built on false pretenses, created by egos of the past.

You have to release who you are not to grasp who you are. It's okay to change directions and let go of previously held assumptions about where your life should be leading you. Often times by not finding our place we seem to find it just fine. Simply put, you have to disconnect from the false to be able to reconnect with the meaningful. Disagree? Well how does one find the time to reconnect in this information saturated age when every single moment of our life is filled with crap that deceives by promising a fulfilling life experience, but delivers only the empty illusion of such? Let go to create space for new, self-guided manifestations to enter your world.

Letting go has to be done in a way that emphasizes respect and consideration towards immediate existence. Manifestations materialize because we want ourselves to realize. Learning what truths teachable moments hold goes a long way toward preventing regret. So be sure to leverage every experience as an opportunity to learn more about yourself. It's critical to come to terms with the "Why?" of manifestations (based on your interpretation) to finally free yourself from what you are subconsciously holding onto. It's absolutely necessary to release all that hinders progress. And if needs be, to move on without closure should understanding become an impossibility at the present moment. Self-exploration is valuable, but not at the expense of forward movement. Eventually all useless baggage will need to be checked at the door to the temple of knowledge that is you.

Just as movement is medicine, concerning the vessel known as our body. When it comes to reconnecting with our psyche, the same applies. Keep moving forward by letting go of what weighs you down. Paradoxically, through our deconstructions is how we prime the pump for putting ourselves together in a way that confirms our strongest foundational elements. Dissecting our current state of existence puts us face-to-face with fears fueling internally violent conflicts. Hindering us with excuses on why we can't live to our full potential. Cut pathetic, bureaucratic red tape and get down to business. Your damn business. A conventional strategy will not help you win your war. You need a guerilla approach. Lighten your load. Thin out your collection of bullshit. Dump your well thought out, lame excuses. There are no valid justifications, when you respect your integrity enough, for failing to realize the potential of your internal availability. This is what will save your ass and get you to where you need to go. By putting ourselves in a position where we are limited to adhere to individual insight, we command creativity that demands the best of us to survive.

Ensure commitment by eliminating ways to wander back. Circumvent recalcitrance by implementing lockstep maneuvers. Permitting only forward progression. Not backwards regression. If options to retreat exist, temptations will be too strong. Powerful enough to sway even the most disciplined. What to do for good measure? When you cross a bridge, destroy it. When you turn a corner, never look back. Fight forward, through your decisions. If there is no rewind button to hit in case of emergencies, you will become a different force.

If we are negatively reacting to something, does it make sense to eliminate the source of the cause or sit down and have a fucking tea party with it everyday? Ironically, it's almost always us who are responsible for all the blocking going on. That is why we have to learn to get out of our own way. It's impossible to say we have done so until we have completely eliminated any and all inconsistencies working against us within our universal fabric. Let go and forgive yourself to begin anew. Get rid of what doesn't represent you at your core, so there's room to embrace that which rejuvenates your spirit. Let go so you can discover that for which you were made. Every step of the journey requires that we release the past to grasp the future. Rid yourself of whatever holds you back, forever.

3.1 : Idealism

Worshiping ivory tower, quixotic details is an ill-fated pursuit. Throughout history such escapades have been the singular focus of many. Precisely why truth has been lost to them. They choose to mold reality to idealistic criteria instead of coming to terms with the universal laws of truth, presented through hands-on experience. Whether ego or its subsequent fears are to blame is irrelevant. Idealistic pursuits distance us from opportunities to understand more basic aspects of humanity. Most importantly, how we can live to realize a more humanized society by first coming to terms with the reality of our own lived experience.

Nonetheless, breaking oneself against the pursuit of an ideal can teach truth. Unfortunately only after wearing down our hard-nosed, stubborn attempts at trying to conform reality to an ideal. By the time we recognize the futility of our actions (by acknowledging what is presented, not what we initially choose to see) we are weakened versions of ourselves. How impactful can we be if blinded to the wisdom that would make us potent leaders of our personal liberation movement? Ignorantly promoting a narrow-minded agenda and only accepting failure when forced. Not very.

3.2 : Expectations

The only one who puts expectations on you is yourself. We are all familiar with the act of outwardly entertaining or secretly nursing preconceived notions regarding results that could materialize before anything actually does. No matter how romantically futile we understand them to be, premature discussions with ourselves seem to happen with great ease. Especially within the preset limitations of expectant minds. Unfortunately, it makes no sense to build complex scenarios for things that are so far only destined to happen in our heads.

Expectations are limiting constructs because you can only perceive to the extent of the context that is you. Nothing more than shot in the dark attempts go beyond. You are better off guessing wildly because life is incredibly circumstantial. We never know what to expect. And when we think we do — surprise!

Expecting is a cloaked act of unhealthy control. At first seeming to empower, this ritual actually entraps practitioners. Predicting what one chooses to believe commits valuable energies in ways that derail the intent of purpose. If expectations are inaccurate, one will still be left with the same reality to absorb; but will be depleted of the necessary vitality needed to do so. Completely exhausted by repetitively working through fruitless reasoning. Subsequently, anything unperceivable will not be acknowledged as a neutral (to be determined) possibility. But as a negative burden because resources were foolishly wasted earlier to establish what has now been deemed inaccurate. Prognostications are at best mildly representative of reality. And for all the misled cheerleaders out there, devotedly touting pompoms in support of wishful thinking, they may want to incorporate these next lines as a staple in their game day routine. As all expectations are unnatural, irresponsible faith is no different. Just happens to be emotionally justified. A different branch of the same tree. Nevertheless, the same shit.

Rules intended to control what lies outside our direct sphere of influence are disguised expectations attempting to safeguard immature, overly protected internal value systems. Such hurdles impede our journey every step of the way. Reality is so unpredictable that I find it hard to follow or make any judgment call about happenings beyond what my actions touch. Even then I'm reaching. The only rules that exist are the ones our freewill limits us to. We must study their drawbacks. Then make a solo attempt to stylishly break them beyond repair. Once and for all.

Getting rid of expectations means just that. Stop creating new opportunities to trick yourself by disguising their presence in new ways. Otherwise you will never be able to get caught up living blissful, individual moments and the profound progress they bring. All we can expect is reality and that is to house no expectations and to continue removing them, one by one, as they appear. Although this realization may feel uncomfortable to those in search of the predictable, know that peace of mind accompanies acts of acceptance. Calmly reminding us we cannot control and are just along for the ride. Accept, relax, work, and enjoy the unavoidable futility of the human experience. That's the way it is baby, get used to it.

3.3 : False Proxies

From an evolutionary perspective, humans fall into the category of Homo faber. This makes reference to our skill as fabricators and creators. The million dollar question surrounding our species' classification: "Are we encouraging the appropriate constructs to enable transcendence for ourselves and the life sustaining organisms which support us?" Most unwanted barriers holding us back are typically put there by us. In the past, mental and physical separations could have indeed been warranted to increase our chances of survival, which is why we still harbor such deeply ingrained instincts. But now? Is it possible that we have unknowingly abused our species' fundamental genius and have begun to erect walls that are unnecessary, in fact detrimental? I think yes.

Why do we build barriers between ourselves and the things that connect us to our core? For what reasons has humanity come to prefer diluted versions of fulfilling experiences? Instead of the "real thing" more and more people are choosing to live through representations. Thereby experiencing compromised, self-limiting realities. The curse of living through representations is that they share many of the same negative qualities commonly found in protection shields. They don't allow us to confront fears completely and solemnly. Just as building protective barriers to our fears never helps us confront them, erecting false proxies to our reality never allows us to fully experience. So why the distance from real? Would we not enjoy the unrestricted freedom that comes along with putting "it" all on the line, win or lose? Or is the safe distance to avoid compromising a bullshit identity that lacks credibility from having never been tested? Either way, release yourself from the illusions of existence and return to your true balance by eliminating compensations. The descent to a simpler, realistic lived experience is very fulfilling. I think you'll be quite surprised! Riches to rags all the way baby! Woohoo!

False proxies are reality avoiding, self-created barriers blocking access to what we really want. We create them because they are the laziest connections we can maintain with certain facets of life without confronting fears. They provide evidence of flaccid connection, but bear none of the inherent risks or rewards of connecting completely to experiences. They are safety nets created to avoid risk and in the process guarantee we almost certainly avoid authentic joy. I believe false proxies are positioned between reality (what we want yet fear) and lived experiences because sometimes a better tomorrow seems so far away we doubt ever reaching it. Skepticism is natural and healthy. It helps keep our ego in check. Especially during demanding circumstances. However, when we are ready to move forward removing intermediary buffers becomes essential to our liberation. Continuing to live "padded" we remain bound by fears and retain the title of "Reality's Bitch".

If your life consists of spending time and energy commissioning a false proxy tomb for your identity, then that's all you'll have. A cold, concealed life where you might as well adorn like a tombstone to blend in with impending mortality. Why limit interactions with

3.3 : False Proxies

unchecked fears? It does us no good. To move forward we need to initiate confrontation. This can only be accomplished by eliminating the delta between the experiences we seek and the reality we are challenged with living.

Modern life is lived in the company of many false proxies that restrict one's ability to experience additional fulfillment. Existing through them, human senses become dulled and ultimately limited prematurely. Far before reaching their maximum potential. If not addressed, this drug like dependency eventually amputates our spirit and condemns us to live like an addicted junkie who cannot confront reality without a fix.

Only—let me reiterate—only delve into proxies for which there is a desired, self-documented return to reality. If a proxy is futile in its efforts to connect us with exactly what it is we want, then it is false. Eliminate that which leads to the disintegration of your soul and eventually the ruthless execution of your spirit. Moving on requires removing what is holding you back. Get rid of unnecessary barriers created by your fears. It's not about dumping everything that is you and making a beeline to safety. It's about building a life that is in alignment with your transitive, ever-evolving self by confronting what frightens you. There are many levels of connection to be experienced, but the purest require no proxies at all. Such experiences await us at our passions' humble and minimal beginnings.

3.4 : Self-Documentation

With perseverance we become intended manifestations. Then we need nothing, want nothing, and are on. Actively anticipating whatever is next. Bright-eyed and steadfastly aware. Cool!

We manifest because we seek something greater. Growth toward this "greater" is an active process of sewing humanizing aspects of our lived experience to our universal fabric. While simultaneously and discriminately unstitching what is geared for lesser human qualities. What we master becomes self-documented and can be let go of to create space for further manifestations and subsequent explorations. Components having yet to be codified consume energy and will eventually need to be eliminated if the prospect of their integration becomes an impossibility.

Our universal fabric is constructed by mindfully stitching valuable elements together. Picking and choosing what resonates within us from our lived experience buffet. We must be acutely aware of what we assimilate and what we eliminate. In order for knowledge to become an accessible and reliable resource in our repertoire we must exercise its various independent components until they become second nature. Fused to instinct through sufficient relevant experience. Nomadic knowledge is the highest level of this integration. Referring to information that has become an integral part of our knowledge base. Available whenever and wherever we find ourselves.

As knowledge is assimilated (becomes nomadic) we become increasingly familiar with our mindset's logics and their respective associations. This occurs because nomadic knowledge is the bridge between loose structures that guide us and tight toleranced, internal protocols necessary to follow through with action. As we continue to challenge ourselves, transcending the mundane to reconnect with the inner workings of our soul, previous encounters become self-documented standard editions within the automatically available library that is us.

Conscious realization occurs after subconscious manifestation. It has to if we live absorbed in the moment! We naturally gravitate toward and manifest clues as to what we want before we even realize. Every facet of your life represents your subconscious condensations. Good or bad. The rate a manifestation can be self-documented (consciously assimilated or eliminated) cannot be accelerated beyond the organic pace and natural course established by surrendering our agenda to stay connected to an experience. Nor should it be. The process occurs as follows. First we manifest. Then through intense codification our conscious sensibilities catch-up. During documentation we become aware of subtle nuances. Reflecting upon experiences and sensations felt during. Once we holistically understand what has been manifested, why it has, and how all is stitched together within our universal fabric; rest assured that it is time to let go faithfully and trustfully. As we continue self-documenting experiences, born of manifestations, it's important that we constantly create room for new avenues of possibility to unveil themselves. Doing so will ensure our journey remains freshly populated with ample opportunities to flourish.

3.4 : Self-Documentation

We sew ourselves to the rest of the world at the edges of our universal fabric. What is always in question is how strongly have we sewn ourselves to it and of what integrity is our thread. When one's fabric begins to reveal tears often it's because the seemingly solid stitching they did early on, during foundational construction, was either not the result of their work entirely or empty stitches driven by someone else's needle altogether.

So I ask you—expecting absolute honesty—is your universal fabric a rich tapestry of experiences where you have thoroughly tested yourself and know the benefits and feelings it brings? Or is it a disposable napkin whose cheap, matted paper is barely held together by unconquered fear and regret? You can lie to the world, but never to yourself. Deep down we all know the truth and that is why we are the only ones capable of setting ourselves free.

4 : Universal Truths

Universal truths are written in the heart of man. Available to all who survive the necessary trials and tribulations (required criteria) to become self-actualized, humanistic individuals. To reach truth, challenge your current belief system. Strip away misleading inconsistencies. Eradicate behaviors blinding you from harnessing the spectrum that is your full potential. Ultimately, to cultivate faith, you must be honest about why you are doing so. Clue. If it's only about you, struggle you will in finding motivation during very difficult times.

Everything surrounding our existence is part of a larger infinite fabric. Never seen in its entirety. Sewing our humble little patch to its indisputable truth requires identifying a connectedness binding all together. By retracing the paths of previous lived experiences and relating similarities of knowledge (gained through self-discovery) we thread our needle with the ability to stitch us to this benevolent life force in a meaningful way.

Nothing assimilated into our knowledge base is immune from being challenged and unlearned. For truth can reveal itself in more ways than one. Armed with knowledge born of truth, ninety-nine percent of our previously held assumptions become inconsequential and irrelevant. Relearning commences.

Just because we believe something doesn't make it true. That is why we must submit to truth as presented. Not as wished. When it comes to cultivating deep sincerity within ourselves, external checks and balances are useless indicators in verifying internal honesty. We are the only ones who know if we are pure in our privacy or just bullshit artists. Cunningly working on another worthless masterpiece only when under a watchful eye.

Remain truthful every step of your journey otherwise you will not trust the next. If you don't build your foundation from the honesty of your intellect and with respect for the reality you experience, you only lie to yourself. The dominating principles in the universe are simple. Only our struggles to go against them are complex.

4.1 : Reality

I have no master, but as truth is my neighbor; reality is our ruler. Let me ask you something. Does it make sense to respect the imagined or the actualized? That depends. Do you want to confront what ruffles your feathers? The journey is about confronting your fear of reality's truth and coming to terms with what is uncovered. That's it. From there erect an existence on solid, stable ground. One from which steady growth is possible. The price tag? Remaining connected to reality by accepting its face value no matter what the cost.

    Establish a healthy relationship with reality by letting go of the controlling power you attempt to exercise over it. This means getting rid of preconceived notions. Stop dictating what you would like reality to be or to have been and accept it for what it is or was. Forfeit exhausting expectations. Humbly accept as readily as truth materializes. Toss ideals that are a waste of time because they go against reality's grain. Get rid of protection shields whose only purpose is to shelter from truth's revealing light. Reality tends to be a foe if one is compensating to avoid it. By contrast, those who do not shirk from the self-crucifying act of confronting what is real position themselves to gain internally forthcoming knowledge about their existence.

The key to understanding reality is existing at the core of experiences and embracing what is found. From this vantage point one learns to trust intuitions and act confidently based on what they discover to be true. The extent to which one grasps the concept of cause and effect will determine the profundity of their relationship with reality.

As we stretch and grow, checking coordinates is helpful in determining whether or not realignment is required. Remaining in sync with reality rewards with the ability to understand what adjustments are necessary to steer clear of disaster and hold course.

Most people run and hide from truth their entire lives. But why? We only hurt ourselves by catering to incessant fears. Ignoring the unwavering forces of the universe, which if we come to terms with can teach us a hell of a lot. You want power? Accept all realities your lived experience comes into contact with and you will command a strength available to all, but harnessed by few.

The firm ground of reality does not exist to destroy. On the contrary. It's a supportive platform, however. If we continue to climb overgrown vines of lies, egotism, false proxies or any other unstable extensions the fall back down to the ground of reality can seem like it is going to kill us. There is only one way to find out. Do what I did — jump! If it does kill you that means nothing in you was real and you were already dead anyway. Nothing real lost, everything fake purged. See, you're okay. Now you can start fresh and begin anew. But beware. Please heed this warning! Resume construction in the realm of bullshit and you are going to have another hard fall. The only one to blame will be you. If you fall again, you fall informed.

The gears of reality spin true. Decide to align your unrealistic, lopsided cog and there will be grinding. No worries. This has to happen. This sacrificial toll funds the right of passage. An invisible badge of appreciation

4.1 : Reality

to be worn in memory reminding you to choose wisely next time around or suffer consequences. Once the teeth of your gear are engaged with those of truth be sure to stay tightly meshed. No matter how difficult, keep the dictated cadence. If you back off and return to La-La Land re-meshing will be just as miserable as before. Hang in there and tough it out champ!

Build a life not upon distant association, but one on sound and truthful reflection. You have to accept reality to experience the value of its truth. Seek to understand what is driving reality to identify guiding principles. View yourself unencumbered by the false. And always remember, you will never come out on top when trying to negotiate with this highest power. Reality always triumphs, whether that works in your favor or not. Reality; it's what is…

4.2 : Nature

We are human first. Before anything else. Regardless of our personal faith, nature is our evolutionary religion. Not this sterile plastic, throw everything away society; evangelized by leaders who have more hands in their ass than puppets. Our souls seek reunion with a naturally organic, balanced lived experience. Precisely why abiding by nature's laws makes absolute sense. Under these tenets the main prerequisite required for survival is action. Uncompromising adherence to the rules of nature constantly pushes us to expand the boundaries of our capabilities. In doing so, closer we come to a holistic equilibrium. For your own sake, decide to live in nature's revealing dirt. As was intended.

Nature is reality self-documented. What we stand for. Where we've been. What is to come. She presents everything we need to know. Open your eyes and look. Beyond what you choose to see. It's all there. Endless parallels highlight our mutually symbiotic duality. That is why maintaining a close relationship with this unmolested aspect of our world provides rejuvenation to our body, mind, and spirit.

In nature human truth is confirmed. Ask yourself, "Based on nature's unerring laws, what makes sense?" Often times humans' interpretation of reality is skewed, because unlike other species we choose how we are conditioned. And typically it does not involve instincts. Definitely not ones independent from the influence of collective social ideals that have become tainted and bastardized. This is why our perversions reveal themselves in ways unimaginable. To live in accordance with nature we must forfeit the belief that it can be molded to our twisted will. Let nature's wisdom be your heart's docent. Come to know the indisputable and infinite truths she seeks to share.

Nature is the greatest artist. Her masterpieces span millennia in a never-ending swath of creation. Unmatched even by God's hand, who may have initially patroned her; but now sits back as we must to observe her continuous miracle. Shame is inevitable when contemplating the evolutionary track of organisms whose fate, in the modern world, is subject to lopsided human discretion. Consider the assignment of consciousness that brings a being to life. To think of personality as a subsequent trait, established at inception, always makes me wonder what miracle I observe; but whose logic will never help me understand. For always there is mysticism. Something cheapened by hard-headed human logic. It's hard for humanity to grasp these gifts because we place subjective value on the flowers of individuality before they ever blossom. Such indexing is not our gain, but our downfall. For all subjectively categorized, awareness accompanying every claim to understand is nowhere to be found. Still, we don't hesitate. I'm not surprised. Most humans tend to be sickly little beings.

No matter how thoroughly invasive society's attempts to mask the damage human civilization has done, it's becoming increasingly obvious that nature's demise is directly related to our inner state of decline. How could it not be? We are one in the same! All our roots can be traced back to our relationship with Mother Nature. She is the transitory reflection through

4.2 : Nature

which we discover the impact of our hindering actions. She reveals just how futile egotistical efforts are. How? Because all life experiences among us share the same fleeting transparency of an existence marked by death. A common theme amongst ignorant men is to put this line of reasoning off till tomorrow or simply turn a cold-shoulder altogether. To those who poignantly proclaim the self-defeatist moniker: "That's just the way things are". Go fuck yourself.

When will we preserve obvious connections linking us to this greater life force? When will we institute balance within the context of all life? I hope soon. Let us be students in a world that is our classroom. Then, when we are ready, mentors to all through unique contributions.

4.2.1 : Duality

Man's external circumstance is a mirror to his internal psychology. This is attributed to an existence firmly rooted in nature. No matter man's aspirations in the mental realm, there is always a physical duality to his cerebral manifestations. As a result of this two-way street, a drive for symbiosis constantly exists between the two.

Undeservingly borrowing life's metaphors without experiencing gives no credibility to words. They have not been tested by the brutal reality of action. Making your life a literal translation — in the flesh — of your ideals will go a long way toward moving you forward with confidence. If you want to climb mountains in your mind, do so with your body.

4.3 : Ego

When the word in your head becomes forgive instead of forget, you are truly over something and ready to move on. Only hindsight has the privilege of a 20/20, imperial box view. With this in mind, don't be another pussy-ass Monday morning quarterback calling imaginary plays nobody gives a fuck about hearing. Save your breath. Accept that you are accountable to justify only to yourself. Avoid haters and critics like the plague. Cut them off at their weak knees anytime they attempt to stifle your progress. Show them no respect. I mean it—none. Your focus needs to be internal, so keep it on target. There is no point in outwardly venting your discontent. The only therapist you need to be telling things to is your to-do list. Not only will this approach save time and money, it will actually resolve shit. Ironically our ego is confused, proving in the outside realm when inside is the only place that counts.

In a culture of spoiled bon vivants we all want to be seen as the prize. Super amazeballs and singularly special! But, contrary to our own deep-seated beliefs, we are not. In the grand scheme of things all are insignificant. Each of us is nothing more than a grain of sand in a universe spanning infinite millennia. Realistically, probably less. Much less. The only reason we oppose this line of reasoning is because the star culture surrounding us understands how to entice individuals' selfish desires. You know, these fundamentally flawed weaknesses we all give into (at least most of us). Evolved alongside our complex behavioral system over the course of thousands of years. Being anxious opportunists, star culture cronies exploit such avenues for profit. Such parasitic demons are without integrity. Deceptively circumnavigating reality. Promoting false, unimportant virtues to top off an already full till.

Nasty residuals are to be expected when blindly making impulsive, egotistical decisions that harbor far-reaching, negative consequences. So don't be tempted by the alluring appeal of cutting your demon loose. If allowed to run wild our ego will trick us into swallowing humongous lies. In order to get to the core of ourselves we need to understand exactly what extensions of our existence have been created and are unjustly ruled by our subversive nemesis. How do we do this? We start by identifying attachments. Deviant prosthetics that cocoon themselves beneath insecurities in areas of our lives where unchecked fears dwell. This is why living from a place where fears have been confronted, and the ego substantially minimized, greatly increases the quality of one's entire existence.

The ego seeks all-inclusive bragging rights. It's this never-ending battle to establish subjective superiority that distances us from traveling deeper into ourselves. From exploring the next level of possibility within our subconscious. The ego's overt concern with proving false certainties, and securing its place among them, is essentially a coup d'état aimed at strong-arming undeserved importance. This sense of entitlement doesn't entitle one bit. Decreased is the potency of our hearts. Hindered is our ability to humanize the world to the extent possible. Mark my words. Ego fueled power struggles always promote dysfunctional scenarios that lead nowhere.

4.3 : Ego

It is unrealistic to believe that the ego can be eliminated altogether. It's an integral component of everyone's complete lived experience. How we manage our ego is a testament to how far we've come. What we can do is learn how to keep our dirty doppelgänger in check by confronting reality and ultimately our fears. Testing helps develop the humility necessary for avoiding ego traps of all shapes and sizes. This can prove useful in the long-run if we are seeking to connect with the enriching parts of our character instead of those lacking merit.

4.4 : Fears

When we are conditioned by fears, it's because we support what fuels them. We have to disable and destroy this revolving door of hypocrisy within our psyche. The things we are terrified of doing are what we most need to address immediately. Then and only then is moving forward with our lives even a possibility.

Fears are absolutely painful hindrances to self-actualization, however. They remain necessary components in formulating a well-rounded, challenging accent to our appreciated and desired lived experience. Fears are anything that presents an obstacle we are avoiding. Things that draw out our inability to feel control over the results of an unattempted outcome. They paralyze us from confronting what stands in the way of progress. They undermine our ability to exercise the bastion known as freewill and in doing so create a much larger issue than fear itself. Lack of self-confidence, which in turn diminishes overall self-esteem. Anything other than confronting fears head-on is futile because no amount of alternative compensation will help one overcome the limitations they impose. If given the opportunity to thrive these misfits manifest themselves as worries and doubts that affect our ability to make deep, solid connections within every facet of our lives.

It is what we know about ourselves that makes us afraid. We know exactly where our breaking points lie in wait and tend to shield them because weakness is not a treasured virtue. We can run from our fears, but we can't hide. If we are under the delusion we can burry and ignore them, they will threaten us from becoming our most evolved selves.

Due to limitations stemming from our primitively evolved behavior mechanisms, it's important that we identify the extent to which fears are actually valid. Trust that they exist, but verify their stature. They tend to keep people from doing so much. So let's confirm their gathered power before we succumb to their perceived strength. The resemblance of their resistance is usually enough to keep most people at bay from achieving what it is they really want. The only reason that our fears have any strength at all is because we nurture instead of confront them, which would in turn greatly diminish their power.

One fear that deserves serious attention: meaninglessness. The simple realization that we have not fulfilled and it's too late. This fear puts all others into perspective. It makes you realize that things aren't scary in and of themselves, but in the simple reality that time has run out. You can no longer live what you so badly dreamed of. This is the 800-pound gorilla we must always confront. No matter where along the path of life we find ourselves, because death humbles all quests. Do you want to have regrets at the end of your life? No? Well then get busy living while the getting is good.

We can endlessly nurture fears or can shift focus toward that which fortifies strength and confidence. Thereby placing fears into a manageable category. Eliminating all fears is a completely unrealistic expectation. Revealing just another facet of our inherent weakness: a desire to avoid all discomfort. Unfortunately by doing so we also avoid reality. Truth is not meant to be

4.4 : Fears

comfortable. It's meant to be real. Living and moving forward, regardless of fear, is what shows true strength and forges the solidarity to be oneself—to the maximum and absolute fucking fullest—in spite of difficult situations. That which we are terribly afraid of is exactly what we need to confront today. Before we do anything else in this life. The will power necessary to do so is directly related to our exercise of discipline and fueled by what is in our hearts. Lock horns with your fears and break the cycle. You'll thank me later.

4.4.1 : Testing

You can work damn hard your entire life and never test yourself in ways that directly address what is holding you back from transcending human conditions. This is usually the case. Most people's modus operandi is to compensate for fears by working extra hard in areas that are not even closely related to what they need to confront. Often unknowingly, they are just a single test away from overcoming a challenge that is likely to affect their entire universal fabric in a positive nature.

The main reason to test oneself is to regain self-control from undisciplined parts of our character. Those shielded, sometimes for years (even decades) by a lack of appropriately targeted focus. Just as weather erodes mountains, creating fissures where weak material once existed, a similar process purges our character of weakness throughout the testing process.

The opportunity to overcome burdening obstacles is seized by those who get up-close and personal with their fear's axis. I'm talking close son. A fitting analogy is fighting a close quarters battle—nuclear style—in a space no larger than a telephone booth. And guess what! You are responsible for leading this devastating assault on the cushy, false reality you previously felt entitled to. The time has come to put it all on the line and let the cards fall where they may. Otherwise you will always question whether your fears were half-heartedly conquered. Don't be dissuaded by thinking it's possible to convince yourself otherwise. Your conscious knows you better than you know yourself. Even if you can hide lies from the outside world.

Having strength means accepting current limitations as a starting point for change. This is precisely why self-deduced estimations of ourselves need to be tested to ensure accuracy. Affirming what we believe to be true requires hardship for self-demonstration purposes. Tests reveal and reinforce our deepest, toughest, everlasting qualities. What we are made of. Or in some cases huge gaps where there is work to be done so we won't fall apart during difficult challenges. We strengthen our universal fabric by stretching it when we test ourselves. Doing so it will either withstand or rip, at which point we know we have work to do. Initially felt is pain. Don't despair. This only temporarily predicates blissful liberation to follow. Trust me. If you make it through, you will feel good. You will feel real good.

Testing is a purification ritual prescribed by Dr. Reality. To survive, one makes it through suffering by shedding unnecessary links to fears. As the age old adage goes: no pain, no gain. You have to become a different person to survive. That is the whole point. You must let go of who you were and move on or remain stagnant and let the virtues of your spirit rot. If successfully traversed, this right of passage leaves one with less dictated drawbacks as a result of facing fear and more forged confidence to once again advance in spite of life's frequent and unpredictable turmoil.

To know you are testing yourself is to exist outside your element. Think fish out of water. Uncomfortable, scared, tired, and any other undesirable emotions self-preservation has naturally drilled into your instinct to avoid. Basically let's see how you do under "less than favorable" conditions. Where you are caught off-guard

4.4.1 : Testing

and your A-game hasn't had a chance to develop. Are you still moving forward with your heart on your sleeve, when crawling in the trenches, surrounded by chaos?

Testing is not about hiding reserves or being able to run back to mama and cry. It's where men are separated from boys. Where women are separated from girls. Here there is nothing to fall back on. Except will, desire, and possibly passionate disregard for bullshit. Which maybe why you are putting yourself through this in the first place. Whatever the case, your back is against a primordial wall and you must deliver. You already know you are not going to feel how you want to feel. Keep in mind, you are not being told how to feel. Feel any goddamn way you want. Hell, whatever tickles your fancy. My point is you still have to do what you have to do, regardless. That means biting the fucking bullet even if it shatters your teeth. So fucking be it. No matter what music is playing you're going to have to dance. So why not choreograph character. Doesn't it make sense to empower feelings that will be productive and supportive to your cause? If you wait to feel a certain way before doing things you will always be working through an internal gridlock, traffic jam of a mindfuck. Please, don't put yourself through this. It's just as painful to experience as it is to watch someone you care about self-inflicting this disgraceful embarrassment upon themselves.

Embrace uncertainty and forced newborn awareness of being a student, a newbie, a beginner. These are exciting times requiring an open-minded attitude. Can your entitled ego handle feeling like a rookie? Anyone exhibiting character during such trials deserves a high-five. Why? Because, they are earning confidence one sacrificial step at a time. What you are really asking yourself during a test is how you handle situations where you are not capable of hijacking the title "Mr. Quick Study". Those in which you are still wet behind the ears and greener than grass. Those in which failure is the most likely possibility if you can't pull your shit together with the quickness. Learn to love this reality and your only limitation will be your imagination.

Great labors of the world are built on suffering and sacrifice. Many who have moved human progress forward have lived painfully turbulent lives. Gladly in fact. Even at the behest of cruel criticism and unwarranted ridicule. All have a burden to bear. An especially heavy bastard if they are civic minded. Some days it gets so hard there's no choice but to bring out the rulebook. It's times like these that force us to deduce exactly what is necessary to survive. At any and all costs. Even then there is no guarantee of success. You want a guarantee? Play it safe. Go be an ass-kissing peon and secure yourself as a step in someone else's ladder. Have fun and don't forget to not write!

Failure is and always remains the most predominate outcome—as it must. Otherwise everyone would be amazing with no effort. What a squeaky-clean little lie of a utopia that would be. I say burn it to hell. Don't be deterred by this crap. Your heart will be able to live proud regardless of the end result if you can sincerely tell yourself you gave it everything you had. If and only if you left every ounce of effort in your utilitarian heart on the table. Failure under such a circumstance is never something to be ashamed of. So long as you get up, dust yourself off, and give it another go. You'll have your respect and that's all that matters. Fuck what others think. If people are criticizing what you are doing and not focusing on their own shit, then they are wasting their time on this earth. Don't let them waste yours. Invisibly communicate a "Fuck you!" Don't concern any amount of your spirit's energies or your focus on these scared safety monkeys. They have plenty of shit coming their way if you are their main concern.

Circumstances reveal man's character or whether he has none at all. We don't learn as much through the easy times as we do during hard trials. As long as you

4.4.1 : Testing

give your all there is never the possibility of coming out a loser because you learn so much about yourself whatever the outcome.

Disillusion falls not on brave shoulders who attempt endeavors with a full heart and give their all till the tank is empty. Lessons of suffering are never in vain. They teach unparalleled humility and respect for the basics. They forge confidence harder than tempered steel. Not to mention ultimate self-reliance. I've always felt melancholic while reflecting upon times like these. Not because they were composed of difficult experiences I regret. But because bittersweet emotions accompanying my reminiscence remind of when I was giving my best for someone other than myself. I chose to do it for my fellow man. That means you. I will miss these "good times". There's no greater gift to humanity than serving yourself in a way which will later come in handy to serve others. Never forget this. We all need each other to fulfill the goal of humanizing the world. You'd better find reasons to make it about others or you won't.

Testing yourself opens the playing field to understanding honest, legitimate parameters that objectively monitor when your level of effort is suboptimal. Tests are what you let yourself experience. If you go easy, by doing the bare minimum just to get by, you pretty much guarantee reality will kick your ass if you are ever exposed to it for any length of time. However if your repertoire includes regular voyages into deep water, where survival becomes a sink or swim situation, you command the best of yourself. Stand tall.

Welcome to the real! Swim in the ocean of arcane risk. Encounter uncertainty to have a chance at reaching deeply buried treasure before life's breath escapes your lungs. Don't let the "Do Not Swim" sign, put up by fears, deter. Unleash bad intentions! Slip and rip internal demons against your bare knuckles! Keep your composure and continue into the darkest shark infested waters humanly known. The good news? Control fear and confidence skyrockets as a result of heightened concentration. Channel anxiety into energy directed toward completing that which you must. Stay cool. Don't lose your shit or you'll regret it. If by chance you back down, when excuses pay your conscious a visit they'll torment till the end of what seems to be eternity. You'll wish you'd done otherwise. But hey. If this happens, maybe it's how you need to learn. The good ol' regretful hard way. Just don't make it a habit.

A factoid worth mentioning. The moment you start making up excuses is precisely when you should push harder. A substantial amount of humans caloric intake (roughly twenty-five percent) is required to fuel brain function. This means that those extra calories you burn while coming up with bullshit could be redirected and productively applied. Your welcome!

Trust that you will rise to the occasion at a time when most retreat. It's their fault they let their fears get the best of them. Don't be one of these safe queens. Acting like scared curators to lives they never had the balls to live. Get out of your safety zone. Throw yourself to the wolves. Cut your teeth on something big. Something worth dying for. Go above and beyond the call of duty everyday for that life sustaining, daily dose of excitement. Put yourself in a place where you risk being killed every time you absolutely must hit a high C note and you will sing a tune more beautiful than can be found on any platinum album. The alternative? Take the scenic route. Let yourself be a passive passenger entertained by external bullshit. Your performances will be flat. Hell, if that's what you want, so be it. After all, this (America) is a freewill country. Right?

It's impossible to know what is going to happen, but I'll tell you one thing my friend. If when the gate opens, the game starts, the bell rings, you are not the one to throw the first punch and turtle up; emotions you feel upon reflection will dwarf those you would have experienced had you stood up to your fears. We're all scared.

4.4.1 : Testing

Guilt can be reconciled through action. Fear never goes away. What does diminish is your reluctance to confront. For demonstrating courage you should be proud. The journey is about responsibility and obligation to your higher purpose. It doesn't matter how you feel. Make the walk all the way down to your primal fears.

Outcomes are always influenced, for better or worse, by how one chooses to act. Those who tenaciously face adversity are unofficial mentors to us all. How will you choose to act? Well, according to this book there's only one way to find out. That's right. Talk is cheap, action priceless. So if you are going to test yourself, then really dig in. Although anything is better than nothing, at least have the fucking decency to go all-out. Tests are meant to be draconian—an excessively tall order. Not Sunday strolls in the park, with mama holding your hand, while you fiddle omnisciently in your little world. Don't fuck around by giving a half-assed effort that harms you alone. Cause we don't need anymore wannabe pretenders. The world has enough of these pansies and keeps breeding more by the thousands.

Testing reacquaints us with nature's laws and reduces our ego because we experience the harsh futility of our existence by way of mental frustration and physical pain. Placing finishing touches on our character to be. Confidence, not egotism, is built upon experiences that push us to discover unknown limits in these new arenas. Here we confirm our identity by existing as that which demands it. As a testament to our integrity we must remain in this zone until we have developed the instant ability to confront, without hesitation and at any time, what earlier paralyzed us. Let's call this an exercise in discipline that will be repeated until you no longer have to remember what I am talking about, because it has become second nature.

Testing is about exposing yourself to various and simultaneous difficulties. Then recovering to face them once again. Until you overcome. When you can be exposed one hundred percent of the time, consistently and with the same results, the test is over. Facing such has now become a standard, self-documented component of your universal fabric. What once seemed monumentally challenging is now just what you did on Tuesday. This is what you do. Regardless. Period. Rain or shine. At this point luck is a long-forgotten factor. Job well done! ¡Olé, olé olé olé! Now, don't celebrate too long and not without demonstrating moderation. It's time to move on to the next challenge before ring rust starts setting in. Oh yah! Once you test and strengthen your weakest link, another takes it's place. That's why you always have your work cutout. Let me tell you something very special. Very secret. Learn to love fear and it will be your best friend throughout any test. In fact, if you want to transcend, consider it your BFF. Forever, forever, forever.

We don't pick the days, good or bad, but we do decide how we act. Everyone is a champion when the sun is shining, but it's not the easy times that build the character we are looking to develop. Let us test ourselves to cement who we are when things are not going our way. This is the only time it matters whether we act like the real deal and deliver on the goods or are just fucking crybabies who can't hack the reality of hard-earned experience. Burdening the world in additionally unnecessary ways. I know which I am. Which are you? Should you decide to challenge yourself by committing to the most masochistically difficult, but positively life-altering actions you can conceive of; my hat is off to you. Much respect. The beauty about testing yourself is that by doing so you gradually build the fortitude to overcome each and every one of life's challenges. Get out there and show the world what you got! Before it's too late. Before the vessel loaded with your dreams sets sail into the horizon, never to return. This means now.

4.4.1.1 : Equalizers

Everyone has limits. Cushy ego-constrained, comfort-calibrated limits. Testing requires pushing currently familiar mental and physical capabilities beyond what is thought possible. Expansion of competency in these two equalizers is of vital importance. Yet time and time again people avoid. This is a shame because developing equalizers stands to impact lives in ways most profound. One would think difficulties associated with such tasks are minimal sacrifices compared to the monumental returns investments yield. You tell me. Is the payoff worth it?

What is gained from training equalizers stays with us throughout life. Through thick and thin. No matter what. Knowledge of oneself can be taken away by nothing and no one. Such valuable, deeply woven threads of personal trial embed themselves like holdfasts within our universal fabric. They are undetachable key components of our nomadic knowledge database. Safeguarded and waiting to be referenced upon discretion.

Developing equalizers is much more difficult and painful than just accumulating information, which in many cases doesn't require excruciating hardship to obtain. This critical lack of association with hard-earned experience is the primary difference between lessons automatically gifted at academic institutions versus those painfully learned in the University of Life aka the School of Hard Knocks. In the context of self-actualization, the first are worth less than squat because they are easy to come by. Especially if you have dollar bills. Fortunately—for those of us who earn their shit cause dollar bills are non-existent—no context (hard-earned experience) exists to frame them so they are not respected and subsequently lost. See! Life is fair. The second? To be revered as priceless gems because suffering has created avenues for these lessons to be readily absorbed by unprivileged ears. They ride shotgun. Second to none. Even you. Pass it on baby. This is the truth that will make you a genuine philanthropist and save us all.

Developing equalizers produces unrivaled advantages. Why? Because they require putting in tons of hard work—which, by the way, is a timeless classic because it never goes out of style—done so with the utmost sincerity of our integrity. That means absolutely no shortcuts pal. Equalizers literally "equalize" the playing field between humans, from various socioeconomic groups and differing walks of life, who are seeking to transcend human conditions within their own contexts. This clarifies, but doesn't defend why people cheat in an already rigged rat race to become just another tainted #1 asshole. If this describes your unfortunate circumstance, I would turn and face the music now. Before it's too loud. Before its constant drone deafens your ears to truth forever. But then again, I drag a mean pair of low-hanging, jaw-dropping clackers. I left everything behind to befriend truth. To make it my brother. My assassin. I don't know if we can say the same for you at this point. Can we?

Always maintain integrity so when it comes time to unleash your equalizers it shows. Work fiercely independent. Outside of assistance or advantage. Guarantee the most painfully constructed learning curve

4.4.1.1 : Equalizers

possible by putting the period on things yourself. Hide from nothing experiences provide. Certify your worthiness to deserve the highest possible ROI as a result of extreme effort that almost kills you. Acknowledge current limitations and proceed step-by-step, instead of cherry picking. Ensure a solid foundation, represented by a badge of credibility you can leverage for life. Maybe beyond. Who knows?

When you completely deserve, having honestly invested in your equalizers, reward is a completely different experience. To say such cuisine is unparalleled is an understatement. It satisfies like the first sip of water after crossing a desert with an empty canteen filled with nothing, but the evaporating moisture of hope. A taste so distinctive its lingering memory can be delicately savored for years to come. On your deathbed this taste you will revere. At the highest reserve. One whose flavor never seems to diminish in retrospect. Treat yourself to a healthy, spirit-sustaining serving. Hell! Help yourself to two! Why not? You are the head chef. You decide what gets put into this creation. Follow your internal discretion and set standards accordingly so you can completely enjoy the fruits of your dedicated labor. Others won't even have the faintest clue of the delicacy they are missing out on. Too bad, so sad. The irony is that there is and always will be plenty of this dish to go around. The only rational question becomes, "Why are so many people starving for it?" Maybe its because they haven't accepted the responsibility of writing their own recipe. Only time will tell, but don't let time tell you. What does your diet consist of? Bitching or work?

4.4.2 : Perspective

Life is not too hard. *Au contraire, mon frère.* We are too soft. Our bodies and minds are so much more resilient than we believe them to be. But it's our responsibility to access hidden reserves. Value is appreciated in direct relation to the tested range (context) established to frame it. Of the many benefits testing brings none is so important as the appreciation it teaches. Ultra-readily absorbed by a mind baring the fresh imprint of recently acquired humility. Did you do as well as you thought you would? What did you learn? Still think you are the shit? What'd you expect? You are only human. If your attitude thinks otherwise all it takes is a visit beyond your breaking point to put your ego in check and remind you who is boss. Hint. It's not you.

People that don't appreciate tend to be synonymous with lived experiences that are too damn easy. Consequently, they lack necessary perspective. These selfish, gaping mouths await satisfaction; but are unfamiliar with the phrase "hard work leads to humility, which teaches appreciation". According to their snotty palates life is never fair. Duh! Nor is it meant to be to a bunch of whiny sissies who don't understand that you justly earn what you work for. Nothing more. If they don't understand this logic maybe it's because their freewill is misbehaving. If they choose poorly who are we to stop them? Let them grovel. We all make our bed and are tasked with sleeping in it. How do you take your dreams? Sweet or sour?

Do you feel misunderstood? Cheated out of a life you haven't earned? Denied of what you think a birthright entitles you to? Well wake up and smell the coffee. Or whatever "other" potion is required to end your delusional thinking. The world does not exist to wait on you. It's not a record you can play at whatever rpm you deem appropriate. The Spanish languish a sarcastic term on complainers: "*pobrecito*". The rough English translation: "ah you poor little baby". You may expect sympathy from the rest of the world, but don't from me. I'm not a keyboard cowboy. Try salty dog veteran. I have been around the block. I know what it is like to get a crash-course in life and have to immediately swim against the tide, battered and bruised, surrounded by bloodthirsty sharks. Do you? If at the end of your life you are the only one who understands you, be thankful. After all. This is why words like "confidence", "esteem", and "actualization" take on unique meaning when the prefix "self" is affixed to them. Things are up to you. Not parents, siblings, friends, neighbors, teachers, politicians, idols, demigods, deities, etcetera. Don't be a slave to laziness. Be a master at wielding destiny. Your destiny.

We live in a society that would have you believe it has your best interests in mind. Yah fucking right! Everything modern is a skillfully disguised manipulation aimed at conditioning us to think in such a way. With the ultimate goal of placating us even further. An act similar to blinding lemmings. What the dreams sold to you conceal is that the grass is always greener on your side. How so? Cause that is where you can take action to make it so. Or any other fucking color you want for that matter! If it's not the shade you selected from the catalogue you believe you can order happiness from,

4.4.2 : Perspective

don't blame the seeds. Point the finger at the gardener responsible for the patch. Are you going to take ownership? No one else is going to apply for the job of changing your diapers when you are perfectly capable of growing up and wiping your own ass. Just in case you don't know the universally accepted technique is front-to-back, not vice versa. Don't forget to wipe!

Think I am being harsh? I don't. We, as a culture, already command these necessary basics in a variety of areas. Just not within the context of us. Ironically where it most counts. Imagine a car that could only be driven when it wanted to be, regardless of your schedule. Would you buy this jalopy? Humans are so fucking hypocritical! We institute tons of double standards. Toward everything external. Down to the most insignificantly stupid details imaginable, however. When it comes to our inner realm of sincerity, for which we are solely responsible, some how we're magically off-the-hook. We think we are so entitled. So special. We expect the world to change for us. Not the other way around. Ha. Ha. Ha. I hope, for your own sake, you can infer that I am not laughing with you. Humanity's advantage of being higher-up on the food chain is running out do to irresponsible neglect. The day it finally does, I have no pity for those who tortured opportunities within themselves to transcend and evolve. Nature is just. Evolution's games don't change just because humans are laggards. From an objective point of view it doesn't take rocket scientists to reach this conclusion. History alone has proven this outcome. Time and time again with little variation of results.

Constantly reverberated throughout our cultural landscape are cries for more. Star culture imprints screaming, "I want this!" And "I want that!" Nothing but egotistical requests from peons who in reality don't deserve shit. Just like bratty kids in the grocery store. Throwing tantrums to get their way. What I wouldn't give to see frustrated parents slap the shit out of their dirty mouths. All I'm saying is, if cops asked me anything about such an incident my only two statements would be, "I didn't see anything". And, "I don't recall". I have countless politicians to thank for that last phrase.

Right this second people are dying all over the world for reasons that in this day in age make no damn sense whatsoever. Why should the well-adjusted populous have to listen to selfish, small-minded begging coming from pussies who are living on Easy Street compared to the majority of humanity? Dying off by the thousands in some countries—every single day! I bet if we gave someone in that predicament an opportunity to take on what an unappreciative person classifies as a "shitty life", they wouldn't hesitate to jump headfirst at the opportunity. To them our problems are golden presents, accepted with open arms. Even the chance to fail is still an opportunity the way they look at it. So why should society feel sorry for you or I? It shouldn't.

Nobody, especially yours truly, gives two shits (let alone one) about those who don't know how to appreciate cause they've been spoiled. Like planets out of orbit. They spin disconnected from reality. The truth is we have it great. Trouble is we don't see it that way. We are far too busy focusing on what we don't have instead of what we do possess. Do yourself and more importantly all of humanity a favor. Become an individual faction of a new movement I call "Silencing Complaints: saving eardrums one unstated privilege at a time". I'll be your first active member. Where do I sign?

Positive attitudes appreciate no matter how rough shit gets. I'm not suggesting becoming Pollyanna. Or any other mental wreck with no impact for that matter. I'm just saying, things could always be worse. Much worse. Take a walk on the bright side. Millions of miracles permeate every moment. Priceless snippets of perspective come into focus when we decide to open our mind's eye. Clearing ego from the line-of-sight. Here we observe butt naked truth. Nothing false.

4.4.2 : Perspective

Possessions, status, money, and all other popular ego-boosts do not make one happy. The way you feel about yourself, in regards to the entirety of your life, is what brings fullness to heart. Deeper satisfaction begins with landing on the firm ground of reality and earning your keep. So when abundance pays you a well-deserved visit, magnified are its gifts through demonstrated appreciation. When we feel struggle, pain, discomfort, and then welcomed relief. We appreciate what it is like to feel good in the right ways and for the right reasons.

There is always something to be grateful for. If your view of the world is lacking experiences that internally frame this line of reasoning, test yourself until you see light. The alternative is to do nothing and continue trolling in complete darkness. If you choose a path through the doldrums, when you die it won't be any different from your current state of ignorance. For to live is to be awake. To die, deeply asleep. While possibilities to thrive drift past. Unengaged and subsequently unrealized. Lost forever.

Adore grim situations. If you are unable, let testing commence. Learn what life is all about from the ground up. Instead of obsessing about what your life is missing, cherish what you got. I guarantee I have met someone with less than what you have who's still happier because they appreciate after experiencing lessons of life's shortages. If you are fed, sleep in a bed, and are clothed; check-the-box. You have the basics. You need nothing more. None of us do. Appreciate that you already live better than ninety-nine percent of the world. Quit blaming external factors on your insatiable quest for more. It leads nowhere.

There's no excuse to sit back and not execute on changing your life. I don't care what justifications you have carefully crafted to convince the world your circumstances are vastly different from everyone else's. Don't throw people lines of crap contaminated by excuse-abused reasoning. It's insulting. Even though some idiots may briefly entertain your bitchy spews, they don't really believe you. They just pretend to avoid the discomfort of calling you out. Me? I'm different. I'll listen. Then it's your turn. Help me help you. Clear those opinion-infested wax buckets and listen. You ready? Here comes truth.

Real champions deny you the formality of excuse through the examples they are living. Absolutely no complaints are valid. Period. Case closed. End of discussion. If you are part of the struggling (those whose fundamental, basic human rights are being denied). Then my question to you is, "How the hell did you come across my book?" And yes, I will feed you. Something tells me that if you are reading this that you're not part of the subset all of us need to rally to help. Unfortunately we've got our hands tied behind our backs until we figure out salvation on our own.

All want to rush off and save the world. Hey! Slow down for just a sec. What makes you think you can go to someone else's backyard and take out their trash if you can't in yours? Think their laundry will stay clean after your departure? Hell no it won't! By fixing your fundamental flaws first, you'll alter the world you touch. A solidly constructed universal fabric will be able to handle the weight of other's problems after you have trained it to handle yours, but not one second before.

Demonstrate appreciation. If action is well within your capabilities execute without question, excuse, or delay. If you do not, you are just plain lazy. In that case, better beware. Coddling derails self-actualization. A most disgusting self-disservice. No favors done unto yourself go unpunished. Only feed when you are starving. Because you tested and passed. Because you have earned and deserve. Otherwise nourished is ego. I have compassion for the struggling. Beyond that I am not here to play the role of forgiving babysitter (no one is) to those who dig their "comfy" graves. Consciously

4.4.2 : Perspective

sinking the last nail into their coffin. Neglecting to invest the time and energy to become familiar with the laws of cause and effect. Refusing to play by the rules of reality. Thereby making it almost impossibly difficult for the virtuous to do so. Why express sympathy? These cheats have creatively disguised ways to go around reality and suffer at the hand of their own will. Tough shit. Although few, well-adjusted folks that pave their own way don't accept handouts. Keep 'em. We work for our living. We've been there and had to learn the hard way. So have thousands of others who you may not even think twice about. Who have sacrificed room on their shoulders for you to stand a little taller and go a little further. So what's the problem with you? Excuses are wasted breaths to us. Save them for naïve fools with nothing to do. Better yet. Do what you must to survive. Like the people who gave everything, which culminated into various twists and turns throughout history. All the way to this point. Where you now stand today. This instant! So you could carry the torch of humanity forward. Don't let mankind down. Take it and haul ass. If you don't, is it reasonable to expect others will? What other alternatives exist? Relying on herd immunity? Well what if all are tainted due to an overwhelming reliance on acidicly corrosive cultural coordinates ans not a self-True North? Do you see the dangers of remaining ignorantly unaware and not taking control of your destiny in a society that breeds followers? Please tell me you do and confirm it through a course of action.

    One can think of an infinite number of excuses not to go the extra mile and do the extraordinary. We have to find reasons to supersede this pestilent and tainted logic. One thought, in particular, keeps me going after all this time. Actions are opportunities. To pay respect. To exude tribute. To acknowledge the treasure that is life. Every breath is a blessing. Every heartbeat, a miracle. Every step along a treacherous road is another opportunity to share thanks and be grateful. We could die at any moment. Yet many don't give much thought to what they would like to accomplish before their pulse is repoed by the Reaper and the lights goes out for good. Give the best of yourself to say "Thanks!" Do it while the fleeting gift of life is in your hands. If you wait until the eleventh hour, don't expect to be able to stave off seeping regrets that a leaky conscious has puddled you with. In universal time, a human life is equivalent to the blink of an eye. Make sure you ride this short-lived rollercoaster, purpose fueled throttle pegged to the floor, till the wheels fly off in every fucking direction. Reality doesn't wait for slow pokes. Neither should you. Ride on brothers and sisters. Live your dreams and then tell us about them cause we all need hope.

4.5 : Futility

Arriving at dead-ends that could've been avoided leads to regret. Life is wasted if spent working against truth. Regardless of the quantities of energy or time invested into rallying opposite faith. I encourage detours that circumvent pitfalls associated with senseless black holes. In fact, I'm hoping your journey is nothing but. Invest valuable, limited resources where they are capable of synergizing in ways that fuel productive forward moment. Wondering where to start this monumental undertaking? Begin by identifying impedance mismatches resulting from actions tuned to the frequency of hypocrisy. Failing to do so diminishes the integrity of one's pulse. Quickly dissolving intention and diluting potency of effort. It's inevitable.

   No matter how much we strive. The level of intelligence we possess or resources we devote. Actions will be wasted on a lost cause if our primary strategy is to shoot in the dark. Leveraging wishful thinking to acquire targets. Spraying and praying never amounted to anything and is hardly an adequate strategy to meet, let alone sustain, concerted kill brass standards. If what you do does not add up to substance, what does that imply about the value of your life and its contributions to humanity?

If what you are doing is not adding value or just plain making things worse, quit fucking doing. Initiate damage control. Execute a stop-loss by digging in your heels. Continuing deeper into the abyss primes for one thing and one thing only: suicide. This doesn't necessarily imply an instantaneous, climactic end. A popular choice amongst those aching to play the role of "martyr" tends to be that of a slow, lingering demise. Going out "on the cross" is not all it's chalked up to be. It's excruciatingly more painful than the immediate resolution delivered by a well-placed gunshot—assuming, of course, a sufficient caliber is selected. Whatever your selfish poison don't make it so others have to step in and rescue your "forsaken", "woe is me" tragedy. It's shameful and embarrassing. If they have to maybe they should pass on your mess.

Decide to singlehandedly turn your fate toward higher ground by coloring outside the lines. Murder thoughts of low regard. Do not fear repercussion. This form of premeditated genocide is legal in the state of your mind. Don't waste the time of those here to overcome. Everyone, including you, has virtues geared for greatness. Don't let yours spin unaligned. Tearing away within the positive constituents of worldly purpose. Your contribution is not only needed. It's required.

Want big things to happen? Lift large, life-relevant rocks. If you want nothing to occur, the complete opposite will suffice. Even though petite, pebble-sized tasks may make us feel productive; their assimilated impact is not solely sufficient to move our life forward in necessarily important directions. So why is sound judgment the first thing to go to hell in a handbasket when pitted against compulsions geared at managing insignificance? Could an ill-fated god complex be lazily lounging in our subconscious? Maybe it's because humans value false control that requires minimal work to uphold as opposed to truthful uncertainty. Hell, I don't know. It makes sense if one is weak. The latter

4.5 : Futility

has the possibility of draining till the day we die. Whatever the reasons, when people refuse to focus on impactful solutions they experience violent turbulence. Sadly this is always at their own expense. My recommendation? Self-diagnose. Are any of these symptoms present? Are mixed signals disorienting your freewill, ike a novice swimmer at the mercy of powerful underwater currents? Or are you a devoted army lead by a single unmistakable creed? Purposely charting a course placing you directly in the line of your fear's fire. Chanting a motto united by the power of one mission. With a wholehearted glint in your eye letting the world know that retreat is not an option. Not now. Not never.

Objects of misguided affection do not become important because existence is labored into them. Contrary to make-believe, most things don't matter. Think this logic can be refuted? Take into account humans' self-bestowed importance versus the enormity of the cosmos. Still tout your original position? Human fixation matters only because we, as a species, glorify insignificance. Dedicatively worship it through self-fulfilling prophecies of isolated superiority. Let's be frank. Plain Jane since we must. What matters outside of collective ideals acquired through constant social bombardment? At least be able to answer this for yourself. If you can't. Lord have mercy. Whichever one you worship.

Looking outside for what can only be found within glorifies non sequitur, idiotic logic. Can external exploration ever lead to what is internal and singularly special? No it cannot. Futility condemns by way of misguided search. Outside is not in and vice versa. To confuse the two is to become perverse. An instrument of your own oppression. The ego's main go-to tool.

Living projections of reality we find ourselves fighting cloned demons. Over and over again. Time to move beyond diseased piles of self-propagated condemnation by confronting what irks. Forge an existence in the narrow, immediate proximity of experiences that have negatively penetrated your sensibilities. Stifled your pace. Maybe even completely cutoff circulation to the supply of your creative lifeblood. A word. In this case, hopefully to the wise. Work through your shit. Your situation. Your problems. Your realizations. Your issues. Temptations attempting to infect your subconscious are strongest when you are the closest to success that you've ever been. Hold a steadfast course and continue undeterred. Only then will it be possible for you to reach the steps of a temple that teaches enlightenment. The nexus that is you.

By remaining an internally or externally bound prisoner, restricted are endless spring-loaded abilities to confront the very things that provide irrefutable salvation. Fears concerned with self-preservation label this a counter-intuitive prophecy. Fuck 'em. Act before this nothing short of amazing, opportunity of a lifetime disappears. Instead of driving yourself crazy from going round and round in circles. In a manner comparable to caged rodents running in place. No matter how fast they think they are moving, the wheels of futility have isolated their actions in time. The real tragedy is that we do this willingly. Enslaving ourselves within the never-ending vortex of a black hole that is ruled by our ignorance. Even though we all know better than to spin our wheels. Catch my drift? If so, move on. If not, learn how. Another option does not exist.

Humans are social creatures. They thrive on interaction. No doubt about it. Now ask yourself, "Does this behavioral trait suggest constantly drowning others in a bottomless cesspool of ridiculous drama?" Immaturity assumes yes. But, in all reality, the world does not desire hearing each and every miniscule happening. Most likely issues blown way out of proportion. Molehills made into Olympus Mons clones. Venting foolishly pours gas on the flames of non-action. A raging bonfire of inactivity. Surrounded by motormouths who have

4.5 : Futility

figured out nothing more productive than to bitch while hogging the warmth of others sacrifices. This behavior is so fucking common you'd think these walking headaches are earning bonus miles orally. Where do they redeem them? Purgatory? Heaven? Hell? Must be some ethereal place I hope never to visit.

Feel the urge to bitch? Stop! Dead in your tracks. Say whatever it is you were going to say to your to-do list. Put your effort where your mouth is. Actions speak louder than words. So eliminate indiscrete verbosities. Lessons learned down their crisis-lined paths are unhealthy, unproductive, and immature. Finding yourself a passenger on this frustrating rollercoaster means it's time to act hastily. Before your expiration date. After which chance is nil. Dissolved will be opportunities. Lost are guarantees—if they ever existed.

Life. It is what it is. Monumental waste can be attributed to defining that which does not matter. Either way. Grey area trivialities are allergic to objective discernment. Therefore, subjective categorization of lived experiences to be seen as anything other than "elemental" exposes humans' lofty interpretation mechanisms working overtime; but at half pay. Inherently trivializing meaning, whether intending to or not. Disguising irrelevance as noteworthy. The high art of pointlessness personified.

Undigested experiences exist as generic entities. Until, by one's firsthand interpretation, each chooses to smooth their edges. Sanding mindfully with the intention of satisfying internally relevant explanatory criteria. Once modified, relevance becomes particular to its interpreter. What was once unpurposed and modular suddenly transforms once it hits our tactical war room. Here tested affirmation confirms what we believe to be true. The key words here are "tested" and "we". The limitation of our perspective is our own ability to perceive. Arguing otherwise is to wander in weeds. Point in a closed case.

Unlike healthy relationships, built on both party's terms and input, the establishment of personal relevance is vastly one-sided. Individuals' determinations rely heavily on isolated executive decision or at least they should. Conclusive context is painstakingly formulated. Little by little. Piece by piece. Allow me to provide an appropriate example. It requires we visit a period during geologic evolution roughly two million years ago. Close your eyes. Imagine the dispersion of Pangaea. Now hit pause and rewind the process. See it coming together slowly? This is exactly how our referential knowledge base forms. Experiences gradually fusing within the tectonic topography that is our awakened consciousness. Eventually transpiring relevance once seated at the core of our universal fabric. Surrounded by the indelible, monolithic Panthalassa that is us.

Completely rifting are alternative, lackadaisical modalities cunningly avoiding action. They all boil down to a dirty wax that can hardly be issued poetic license. Those who navigate this route eventually summit the unstable pinnacle of mental whorishness. If issues are not being addressed directly, does it make sense to fixate on them or their causes? Resulting in mindfucks warped by a skewed reality and gangbanged by bastard conundrums, born of action-less mothers. Slutty, cyclical patterns of raped overthinking. Unless frivolous rationality is linked exclusively to executables, guaranteed uselessness ensues. We are responsible for doing. Let's not further intoxicate demons creatively while driving the Devil's Turnpike, ego-drunk on a spirit labeled "Semantics". A name by any other name is still a fucking name. Disregard impotent forms of mental masturbation that never culminate in conception. Less thinking. More doing.

Not to sound too much like a misanthrope but what entitles privileged, low-browed, egotistically endowed, results-lacking individuals to assume they singularly

4.5 : Futility

hold keys capable of unlocking massive global change? Are they state's evidence representing this unproven theory? Please, do your personal self-actualization movement a favor. Memorize the term "bullshit artist". It has profound applicability. Especially this day in age. An era when so many bozos seem to know way too much about what they cannot do or have not done. How the fuck are they supposed to show you "the way" if they don't even know it? It can be quite revealing, from a credibility standpoint, to confirm whether solicited advice harbors roots in actual hard-earned experience. Better yet. Are claims accompanied by desired results or lackluster manipulations of tainted truth? You're your greatest the fact checker. Do they?

Ask those who confidently attempt to wear the shoes of "guide" to share their curriculum vitae. Qualify the dirt on their trail. Did they walk a cleared path, then all of the sudden pepper it with pseudo-proof? Intended on fooling everyone, particularly themselves. Reminds me of those who pursue agenda-disguised philanthropy, but end up unveiling true intentions because they request praise at the top of their lungs. Impossible for anyone to ignore. If you want go ahead and trust, but verify your inspirational inclinations. Have the self-proclaimed sages, elbowing their way into your ears, accomplished under respectable conditions? Are there hints of could-be relevance to milestones you are targeting? Most importantly, was their starting block bolted down where yours was? If important proof is missing chances are these self-crowned profits haven't done shit. Don't adjust your speakers and do not pardon my French. You heard me right.

Fuck being a sport. Do not give them the benefit of your doubt. Even if they are on their fucking hands and knees begging like dogs. Instead watch them drown in lies while you secure the nearest soul-saving, flotation apparatus around your existence. I withdraw respect at the first sign of inconsistency. What do you do? I'm only asking cause dots of credibility are supposed to connect, through the linking of relevant experiences. Let me take a wild guess. Important details are vague or missing from the storylines of gurus you pay attention to. Their learning curves probably have more holes than can be calculated with multivariate mathematics. With massive amounts to share, their talk should be commensurate to an equally impressive walk. If it isn't, extend your finger. You know which one.

Do you gather advice based on the sole criteria of only accrediting those who have honestly trekked to similar places you wish to go? All I'm saying is, qualify prospective mentors. Put them on notice and under glass. So you can finally realize I want you to follow as few as possible. Preferably none. Did they start from the bottom step of the first floor or did they take the elevator up the first few flights of their learning curve? Shortcuts condemn. They short-list could be resources. Quickly disqualifying those that should never be referenced. Believers of experiential handouts beware. Cautiously qualify the tainted plethora of advice you risk receiving anytime looking outside yourself and heed this warning. Beyond your conscious rationalization there is no reciprocity in a world trained and rewarded for disguising self-interest. Go-getter narcissists try so hard to appear sapient. Synonymous with uncircumcised hypocrisy is a more fitting description. Funny how it never crosses their minds that they are the problem replicating. Forget cutting just their foreskins. I say cut them off completely. At their fucking knees! Then properly dispose of their remains by throwing them under-the-bus. Fact only equates to trust when safely homegrown for garden-to-table consumption. By you. Only you. Always and forever. Everyday in everyway.

It is impossible to positively steward the future if we do not address and overcome challenges hitting home first. Something pathological fucks claim to have done, yet are cleverly living a disguised lie. Pompously showcasing false authority. Keeping reality at bay because a single surface scratch would bring down their entire house of cards. Transcendence equates to minimizing, with the ultimate goal of someday eliminating, our taint upon humanity. Responsibility to eradicate hypocrisy falls on all shoulders. No matter how broad or narrow. A good start in eliminating this delta? Not listening to wannabes and not becoming one. Get it? Got it? Good!

    Be completely aware of what constitutes futile effort. Not only in terms of personal development, but also within the context of larger societal collaborations. This is of paramount importance. Ensure actions have a chance to decimate intended targets. Lest they be neutralized by the perils of limited foresight. Make life easier for yourself and the rest of humanity. Fight to win. From a place where your existence is allied with actions that lead to positively measurable outcomes. Not to lose. Where goals secured within your right hand encounter nullifying opposition resulting from the hypocrisy shaking hands with your left. Unite both to empower a common cause. Balancing divided agendas accomplishes squat. Attempt it and fail. Stuck you'll remain. Stranded. Sequestered. A hopeless resident of desolate wasteland. Flanked by indecision and compromise. Do say I warned you.

4.5.1 : Privilege

Privilege is the heavy-handed father of ego. Imbued in all things impractical. Completely undeserving of respect and as limiting as it gets. If this describes your particular upbringing—boy—you're in for a rude awakening. Why? Because your learning curve will likely be jagged, snaggletoothed, and littered with potholes due to a lack of sacrificial investment. Trust me. Nothing that a firm, hard test won't confirm. Opportunities exist for everyone. Accessible to all, dependent of course on attitude. Privilege can seldom be counted on to provide anything other than long-term hindrance. As self-actualization is not a team sport with you acting as the unparticipating, overbearing coach.

Privilege coddles, as would a subservient slave. Agreeing to do "dirty work" so you can shine. Even when you aren't yet worthy of polish. Thereby allowing avoidance of critical learning curve components. Opportunities, on the other hand, permit just enough necessary runway for endeavors to be developed into outcomes. Nothing more. Opportunities abound. The problem is that being a culture of spoiled, recitative golden children we ponder great feats. Committing to action only where it's easy: in our imaginations. Meanwhile awaiting the perfect storm to commemorate our inaugural start. Discriminatingly cherry-picking all avenues as possible candidates for a chosen path of least resistance. Such behavior begs the question, "Why not make due with circumstances provided?" After all, opportunity is chance. Crappy or grandeur. Miniscule or massive. If this is not clear please confirm your definition of an opportunity is not being confused with that of a privilege. A common hang-up is identifying with the proud ideologies of opportunity, but in actuality relinquishing oneself to the role of an expectant beggar. Panhandling armed with misguided criteria causes endless chances for change to be blatantly ignored. Initially starting to rot in the gallows of the unaware mind, chances then become completely spoiled when they gain enough momentum to spiral down the drain of an all too familiar wasted life. Seeking privileges never fuels desire. The pursuit negatively vaccinates against survival-oriented creativity. Leaving all inoculated developmentally challenged. Be honest when you need a firm hand. Avoid drawbacks and put in the work. It's that simple.

Prepared to swallow a tough pill? Keep in mind, you can resist and make things difficult or ask for it on the chin and get it over with. Ah, the presence of the essence of fear. To get what you want you must be willing wrestle with things you don't even want contact with. Otherwise you will inevitably feel discord amongst your emotionally summoning ranks. Dichotomies for which privilege shields a safe bypass. Worthless mental trappings that castrate search and seizure abilities. Appreciate by extracting opportunity out of every pore. By distilling it's potency from blood, sweat, and tears. When you struggle, dedicate self-crucifixion pains to what you love. Actions aimed at greatness are never suffered in vain. No matter how small or of what quality.

Never plead clemency when convicted of a past marinated in lack of awareness. You acted. Whether you realized it or not. You exercised freewill. Shit does

4.5.1 : Privilege

not just happen. Somehow we are always responsible. So don't bitch if you find yourself unsatisfied. Learn from mistakes. Reflect on discord. Fine-tune judgment. And move on.

Life is the occasion. How do we mark it? We exercise prudence. We maximize potentialities. Blue blood germination in a static bubble, compartmentalized a safe distance from reality, is not opportunity. Ha! Ha! It's an evil double D size booby trap that sucks you into an alluring, but deceptive,s ocular scam. Do yourself a favor. Figure out how to overcome human conditions affecting your life in real-time. Just like everybody else. Sans a silver spoon. It's not the arrow, it's the archer. Think organic. Think basic. Off you go. Now make it happen.

Screw unnecessary advantage and its entertaining court jesters. Teach yourself humility through hard circumstance. Lest you too become an unappreciative, weak little bitch. No gifted respect or compassion for people that encounter unwanted byproducts as a result of delusional sensibilities embedded by excessive previous fortune. Not having earned is in fact the reason suffering is present. A common case of too much, too soon. Having it easy and leaping ahead of work is not all its cracked up to be. So why should society endure the burden of another emotional tax? Obliged to feel sorry for those that suffer at the mercy of their own previous comfort. Compassion in this case makes no damn sense whatsoever.

While I'm still on this thought, fuck nepotism! Plain and simple. It shifts ones life into higher gear before their engine has been tuned to turn. This is why walking before running is a concept stressed over and over in relation to learning curves of all different shapes and sizes. Accepting a gradual load acquaints beginning practitioners with the tools to eventually take a crack at becoming a real top of the heap, crème de la crème badass. Baseline fundamentals that instill fairness as ultimate virtuosity. Noble battles ensure legitimate champions are naturally decided. Olympic competitions are not predetermined, nor handicapped. Medals don't go to those who have been collectively selected to receive based on subjective criteria. Albeit sometimes they are misawarded to cheats, but my point is that they rightfully belong those who deserve wholeheartedly because they have earned. Forged the path to claim greatness by their own hand. By recognizing the selectively-separated—those born in troughs filled with advantage-fortified nutrients—cascaded are lies disguised as a series of miracles accessible to common men. In doing so, discredited are gut-wrenching performances synonymous with the struggles of unsung heroes. Marginalized are those who at a first glance might not look like anything special but are in fact warriors who clawed, scratched, and killed to get where they now reside in honorable memory. Starting entirely from a non-existent birthright. Show some respect. All you can muster is the least that will do.

A million-millennia marred by unverified rags-to-riches fairytales have lead to the proliferation of current unhealthy standards and in the process raped our often naïve outlook, through attractive yet false exclusivity. Privilege can be engrained at such a cellular level that habitual perpetrators of its falseness rarely realize the ease with which they spawn useless, ethereal anthologies. Collection after collection of decayed ideologies, packaged to appeal. A far cry from this production-line bullshit, equitable knowledge is born from scratch. Entrusted to guardians encouraging start-to-finish credibility. From initial inception through complete maturation. Requiring purveyors of such to surpass reality's pace by running alongside it. Then, when they've earned the right, efficiently reflecting. All the while slowly observing the current moment tracing their path back to them. Then they're up and running with the pack. Addressing common responsibilities once

4.5.1 : Privilege

again. Except for the brevity of intermittent moments, no one who desires maintaining relevance may ride life free of constraints for extended periods. First-class window seats on the train of privilege have nothing to share, but tainted observations of reality. What atrocity is to blame? The all too desired comforts prevalent in climate controlled, advantage-padded compartments. Further enhancing an already smooth ride. Sounds pleasant, but I would rather die in the cold. My eyes starring into the uncharted heavens. Vehemently proclaiming, "My transcendence is worth more than mere creature comforts and false security." You?

The non-modestly cultivated consequentialists think results reign supreme. That the end justifies the means. Regardless of sins committed to achieve. Collectively implying that it is acceptable to sideline higher ethos. Wrong motherfuckers! Roads paved with lies and half-truths perpetuate that which is inaccurate and irreplicable. Propagating unfairness in the form of manipulated entropy. Attempting to secretly banish truth beneath a cloak of translucent shame. Thereby allowing those guilty to abandon fatherhood responsibilities with their malevolent and hideous bastard creation. A standard never intended to be reached. Simply adorned with unsightly praise that honest men and women should never have the burden of concerning themselves with. Be virtuous. Avoid pedestals that the common man will never sit upon. Let alone stand. Why? Because precipitations of bullshit damage people who just can't measure up while doing right. Smash this glass ceiling and condemn its lethal shards to hell I would. Unfortunately I'm not God. None of us are. So what gives some the right to act like it just because they were born with a better pot to piss in?

In the "Age of the Dollar" classic self-actualization techniques run counter to modern economic principles (i.e. division of labor/specialization). Outsourcing is definitely a means of scale that can be leveraged to provide monetary advantage, however. Enlightenment accepts no substitute for direct, personal involvement. Nor does it trade its riches for partial, project management participation where deliverables are account for on someone else's watch. Why should it? Such is pathetic and should be rewarded as such. Every second that ticks away is an opportunity for complete engagement of oneself into oneself. How else can you endure societal bottle shock aimed at vinegaring your vintage? Every juxtapositional stage in this book is an infinite parallel to every moment—of every experience. Hunger primes senses to identify such embedded blessings. Just as starvation can stir motivation to survive beyond trials thought possible, so can desire lead to the discovery of morsels that nourish forward. Creating endless parallels of possibility for those who settle at nothing to quench their soul's salivation. What privilege fails to expose is that life is scattered with unpredictable hungers. As soon as you think you have the answers the questions change. Humans are always in pursuit of satiating another emerging mouth. Why not satisfy our growing pains for good? On our terms. What do you say? Let's hit the spot!

The resounding sound of "yes" is a grandly false comfort to ears seeking approval for insatiable, self-justified desires aimed at improving or securing advantage. But these tenant praises, maliciously formulated at best, bestow inaccessible virtues. Internal greatness reveals itself at the bleeding-edge of your war's front. Where the rubber meets the road and reality is cornered. Where lies cannot hide because they are exposed a thousand times over. Say adieu to backup and don't plan on being saved by the bell. Dare to be different. Set off on your odyssey. Find an ecological, social, monetary, and spiritual niche by living through your experience alone. Leveraging yourself as the only source of inspiration and truth to work from. Plan and execute your exodus. Descend into reality and reclaim

4.5.1 : Privilege

your conquered psychological landscape. You are the genuine article. Therefore your beliefs will prevail if you believe they will. So will the knowledge that the weight of hell on your shoulders may slow you down, but not extinguish your flame's conviction.

Experience creativity-igniting limitations by shunning readily available privilege. If you have none to begin with, even better. You're all set for this voyage mate. The destination? An island where you can practice eliminating hypocrisy till you perfect the art and develop your own style. Desire thrives by being nurtured in such a starved, isolated environment. A setting in which problems are overcome through raw confrontation. Just you and them. No manner of pretend equates to this level. Transcendence ahoy!

Do not ask for permission to be freed from the constructs of detriment. Ruthlessly seize. Do not exploit circumstances that parlay into a position you wish to be. There are plenty of legit opportunities to go-around. So stay away from the easy lay or be subjected to the drunken murmur of a dirty whore begging for a tip following a cheap fuck. Maintaining a pleasurable existence is not a prerogative. Anything of worthy mention concerns change and what it takes to achieve it. Setting unachievable standards is a legal sin. It's cheating, lying, and every other despicable, novelistic idea in the mind of a derelict culture concerned only with self. Those who embrace this ideology, conscious or not, are worthless in the grand scheme of things. Why? Because no decent human hides from real work. That's what makes my proposition accessible to everyone. Not just you.

Hoop dreams allowed to materialize disembowel any possibility of self-actualization. By our own short-sighted opportunism we tend to avoid painful lessons unless forced. Embracing unearned one-ups is simply easier. The trade off is the limit of sentiment that follows initial relief. The reason we feel as if opportunities are out-of-bounds is because we're asking too much as a result of previous conditioning. What we deem a reasonable request is in actuality anything but. Consequentially we become disillusioned pity parties. Pouty, wallowing squatters in a world that just doesn't "understand" us. Or so we think. There is one and only one word for this fatalistic behavior: pathetic. At such a time the only permissible action is to challenge current thinking. Is it possible we could be doing something wrong? Hell, of course it is. Before throwing in the towel is there at least one step that can be taken immediately to move things forward? That my friend is opportunity. No matter how large or small. Learn to spot it and Lady Fortuna will always feed you prior to those seeking unjustified handouts. Recognize traces of light that will eventually lead to the source of brighter possibilities initially desired. Just never forget. You have to toil in the doldrums of darkness to experience transcendental luminescence at the end of the tunnel. Otherwise you will mutate from a respecting entity into another capricious jerk. Tell me, who wants to hear annoying touts of non-existent opportunity from those blind to its presence? Nobody? I didn't think so. Those hideous pleas should remain sequestered for eternity. Like encased rocks amongst the depths of an undiscovered quarry. Impossible for even the most accomplished sleuth to uncover.

Now, let's permanently retire a popular recipe. The "Safety Monkey Quaff". Please. Don't write it down. In fact, vehemently avoid it. You ready? Here it comes. Take multiple breaks when overwhelmed from experiencing what are the common hang-ups associated with life. Whenever you encounter difficulty sprinkle in a little pity and ask those surrounding if you can borrow a cup of sorrow. What's the matter? You don't like the way the concoction tastes? Well, allow me to suggest a modification to improve upon it. When your life turns out to be anything but what you want it to be ask

4.5.1 : Privilege

yourself, "Who the hell do I think I am? Getting off the hook from experiencing what ninety-nine percent of humanity must bravely face or pathetically witness." Think you are special and that your shit don't stink so the world needs to make an exception concerning your situation? Well, are you? Hell, if you are correct me. Seriously though. Honestly is the best policy. Distance from less desirable aspects of what it means to be human doesn't aid internal forces in pursuit. It converts readily available muzzle energy into useless, dribbly ooze.

Now for the kicker. Life never stops throwing curve balls. That's why you have to stay in the pocket and fight it out. Shit storms are always on the horizon. Await clear conditions and you'll never get around to anything. The point is you decide your level of involvement. You decide what you let yourself deserve. If you are weak and indulge at a low threshold-level for accomplishment you will never raise priorities to the top of your bucket list. So if you decide to sit on the fence be prepared to have a sore ass. Life has barriers. That is nothing new. Many of these monstrosities are invisible or unperceivable. Doesn't matter. What are you going to do? Say *anacol*? Cry wolf? What if no one is listening? Now what?

Ignorance courses deeper than bad blood. Insignificance dilutes. Feelings of unsecured destiny suffer any way you summon their executioner. Privileged living takes on many wasteful connotations when observed through unabashed eyes. It just doesn't make any sense to me why well-informed folks acknowledge this and then do the exact opposite. If you know, tell me. I'm curious why.

Expectation is privilege. One does nothing more than undeservedly receive. Just as mail arrives. No learning curve required. Opportunity is cultivated and maintained. Motherly nurtured, as land would be for the necessity of bearing food. Claiming this nourishment implies a cost that people like myself pay for dearly. To us freewill is king. All indispensabilities associated with it deliver empoweredness. Ignoring to recognize reliance makes us feel like we reign supreme. That's what the fuck I am talking about! To ignorant assholes permitted access to unearned basics our plight means shit. They weren't required to endure trials that develop respect. Easy fucking come, easy fucking go. They take everything for granted, while we take nothing and express gratitude through every passionate effort. They lack credibility until they decide it's time and prove it to themselves. Fuck lesser and uncongenial methods from praise. Lest humanity be royally screwed.

Egos require an unfair, competitive edge to maintain. They didn't really conquer the tundras to which they attach their names. Cherry-picking lightweight titles to boost stature. Wow! So fucking amazing! Not. They will never know shit until they stand at a barely recognizable precipice, gasp with fear, and jump without a parachute. A preferred method of training to test the worthy: those tackling life's heavy weight challenges to show these pussies what's up. Don't be an opportunistic asshole by unwarranted, sexy design. Confront the biggest, baddest of your bullies first. The rest fall into line. You'll see. Seek out adventure or you'll become your ego's co-conspirator. Executioner to well-being. Flirting with reality instead of stepping into the foray of truthful, exploratory existence. How grand I would think. Yet how pathetic those who neglect this self-evident prophecy. Fulfilling dreams requires not asking for anything in return. Just claiming for yourself and yourself only what makes one a super-hero: to do as if fearless, even though fear is felt. That's it.

The end of days prophesize immense burden. There's just no other way to look at it without candy coating a bunch of lame-ass euphemisms. Question is, "Are we progressive in understanding how to avoid this kismet?" After all, we are singlehandedly responsible

4.5.1 : Privilege

for our liberation and beyond. Let's not kid. The things going on in this world are harsh, cruel, disloyal, and sick. Adversity and negative shit are everywhere. Avoid privilege's trappings that turn life into a circumventive dice-roll. Shun the idea of being a spoiled gambler. Skill is born of awareness. It is evident that great masters reduce risk through steady-handed precision, which guides their every move. What rookies don't even know they need, masters are excessively familiar with. So now you know. Push the envelope for something other than a shackled, *cursi* existence. Don't write or receive checks that replace efforts. These will eventually bounce in the bank of purpose.

4.6 : Freewill

No matter what your past the future is yours to define. As humans we harness the supreme ability to exercise freewill, within immediate contexts. Whether we choose to or not is another matter altogether. Resurrecting this lost art has to do with remaining non-thinking, non-responsible advocates or deciding to become active change agents. Wielding self-realized power. Acting in accordance with reason. How you'll spend your time on earth is determined by whether or not you flex your freewill. It's the difference between accepting or rejecting reality. Don't blame your behavioral dysfunctions. You control through action so avoid blaming external factors when things do not go your way, as a result of elements within the realm of influential. Man or woman up! Blame internalities, not the outside world.

Expressing freewill means setting off on a quest and be willing to sacrifice whatever is necessary. It is the choice to become master weaver of your universal fabric. Conscious commitment prepares us to access unlimited internal powers, which regulate life. Deciding to ally with these truths is the first sign of accepting responsibility. It shows you have skin in the game and are ready to compete for the title in which the understanding you gain about yourself is the ultimate prize.

Instinct is priceless to one who is free, but worthless to those who don't trust themselves. More often than not, people aren't internally secure because they have not yet landed on reality's firm ground. Consequently they experience unrest when it comes expressing freedom, as they would like to. Beyond rational intellect lie reasons why "hope-ers and pray-ers" relinquish the ability to have a say in the direction of their destiny. Latter blaming external factors instead of themselves. We only lose power because we throw it away. It's not that we can't exercise freewill, it's that we choose not to. I want to make this distinction very clear. We author our fate. We take on responsibility and we relieve it. We determine our level of involvement through commitment. We choose either way. Whether we believe it or not does not matter. We are our master. We are the makers of us. We struggle to the extent that we choose to struggle. If things in our life command us, it is only because we let them.

Freewill liberates from rules created to replace it. Challenging practitioners' understanding of cause and effect relationships. Requiring us to map out personal reactions, with universal forces at play, in the shared-responsibility areas where human interests collide. Don't subjugate yourself to a life that is mediocre. Set yourself free. Follow your intentions. Let your destiny belong to you and only you, my young cartographer.

Living your life is not a draft, but a volunteer army. In many ways this will increase your chance of victory because you recruit desire. Not your guilty conscious through obligation. It's up to us to determine what is right. To redefine meaning, and to accept that we own circumstances. The ball is and always will be in our court. Will we serve ourselves a sentence foreshadowing a barely tolerable existence? Or will we command in new and unchartered directions? Scattered with endless possibilities. Let's see. Live an exciting adventure or roll over and die like an infected mass? Shouldn't be

4.6 : Freewill

that tough of a choice. Ultimately you decide and that goes for everything. Just remember, if you do not take the lead in your life you will be at the mercy of lemmings who will steer you in directions you do not wish to go. Nothing is written until you write it. The pen is in your hand. Just don't claim you never had the chance to write yourself as the conquering protagonist. Here is your opportunity and here it will stay. Unless you decide to do something with it. You have the world waiting. So what are you going to do? Tick-tock, tick-tock, tick-tock...

4.7 : Love

Every journey is fueled by love. To love is to give the highest gift and expect nothing in return. Love is so unique because at any moment the warmth of its memory can be basked in. Yet I caution. Love only continues as far as it is unconditionally gifted. This blessed force begins with allowing ourselves to feel that we deserve it. And to make it a priority to feel it, while gratuitously passing our heart along to others. It's no surprise that you are what you give—the more the merrier. On this journey to learn to love ourselves, in the hopes of reconnecting with what brings out our best, remember. Love not promises of the future, but the current moments reality bestows.

4.8 : Life

Reconnect with what you love because there is an end. Life is about getting in touch with ourselves through the process of understanding immediate environments and the elements of which they're composed. Empowering us to architect a life that constantly tunes us into our ever-evolving self. Life is not about excluding what we don't want. It's about focusing on what we do want and letting the rest of the bullshit sink into the obscure abyss. There is no room, nor time, for the unwanted. Every bit of energy is demanded by higher purpose.

Life will take the form of what we choose. Be it battle or peace. Our ability, or lack thereof, will determine where along the continuum of transcendence we become despondent in reaching the next step. Or whether we courageously leap forward. Life isn't something that can be observed in a state of suspended animation, while extracting stagnant meaning. Regardless of how we perceive it, life is a seamless experience whose constant season is cyclical change. Although it may appear otherwise if we buffer our lived experience through deceptive methods of compartmentalization.

Life is not about enforcing a complex series of justifications. It's about being yourself and existing as you are. It's about living honestly and with transparency to truth—one hundred percent of the time—so you can outwardly live your deep conscious. Immersed in a constant process of accepting yourself as you are. Who you are at your core will never change. Once you realize and accept, the course you are here to explore and share will become unmistakably evident.

We are living from conception till death. Life's variation of intensity (moment to moment) varies greatly by how we appreciate our fleeting gift. For all those seeking safe passage remember. If life weren't a risky proposition, it wouldn't be worth living. That said. Don't forget to see the beauty of each and every stage of the journey you find yourself a part of.

5 : Human Systems

Living harmoniously by design has to do with understanding the mental and physical environments, which constitute our universal fabric. Extensions through which we experience the world. How do we begin to understand the operational complexity of these environments? Systems. How do we create operationally efficient scenarios, which work wonders to streamline all aspects of our lives? Systems. How do we organize and manage the components of our universal fabric in a way that liberates our mental cache for new cognitive endeavors, instead of trapping us? Systems. Transcending through the implementation of systems requires us to understand information flows at an absolute level. When these flows are mapped one experiences information nirvana: a symbiotic dance between the inputs and the outputs of our lived experience. Enabling us to progress by supporting our intended purpose. Designing systems with awareness of the self-documented processes that positively contribute to our universal fabric directly impacts our unique contribution to society.

Everything we surround ourselves with, mentally and physically, is a placeholder for refocusing our attention. Unless it is already integrated into the larger order of how we live. Far too much time is wasted managing what's not had its purpose integrated into our life and should be discarded. Living operationally sound scenarios requires identifying surrounding waste, eliminating redundancy, and decommissioning senseless processes claiming to do the opposite of what they do—complicate.

The advantage of becoming active change agents, deciding how we live, is that we are able to identify which systems suit us best because no one knows what it is like to be us like us. When was the last time you thought or acted in a way that was out of the box? Are you sure? Almost every structure we exist within has already been pre-established. We are really just working within a box where the structure is larger than what our awareness can perceive. Creating playgrounds suited to our best interests requires going beyond working within structures that have been created for us. It is naïve to think of ourselves as "out of the box" thinkers if still working within a bigger box we're not aware of. That said. Create structures you determine to be appropriate. Independent of the generic ones that prepackaged educations and plastic-wrapped experiences familiarize you with.

Most people never live outside the structures that have been created for them even though within their domains they may be seen as "out of the box". They are simply living along a continuum where any discoveries are part of a larger fabric, which contains them. This type of living isn't good or bad, but it definitely isn't independent of influence. And that is what we are trying to achieve. Realize yourself exactly as you are—sans contextual interference—so you can be sure you are looking at the real thing.

The problem with relying on pre-existing structures to guide us is that they house expectations. Many of which can be debilitating if not aligned with what we consider to be reality. Being capable of creating any

5 : Human Systems

structures to live by empowers us to realize the existence we want. Human systems in alignment with deeper purpose maximize the expression of our values to keep us going strong. Such is only a possibility when we have one hundred percent visibility of our universal fabric. This in turn grants us the confident authority to make appropriate systemwide adjustments necessary for forward movement.

The key is to simplify the way we live by understanding how we juggle life and where we sometimes drop the ball. As a rule of thumb, the less we juggle; the less we drop. Observing your natural workflow (as a result of your practiced routines) allows you to take in raw information, which will later be used to piece together repeatable steps geared toward delivering unique value. Being able to experience administrative standardization in daily operations enhances freedom. By empowering our ability to transcend the mundane, which becomes daunting if not accounted for.

Understanding how we operationally live or "flow" enables us to create empowering extensions of exactly how we want to live. And it is all about going with your flow. Not only does understanding how we are wired go a long way toward our improvement. It helps us recognize and relate to the larger societal structures around us and all that moves between them. Human systems, which we are able to live and those that we can come to know, are useful in aiding our understanding of humanity when we leverage them as relational equity variables to extend thinking.

The goal is not to build a system that is perfect out of the box and has every detail worked out. But to embrace a methodology that permits ad hoc adjustment through real-time usage. One that will be moldable through personal fine-tuning. Starting with a working model allows the opportunity to codify processes that create value. Prepping inevitable integration in a way harmonious unity between all can be achieved.

By weaving self-certified best practices into your universal fabric you create an accurate homeostatic, living reflection of who you are. Once you have self-documented process components into your universal fabric there is no need for independent elements working outside of guidelines for the whole. The result is balance on your terms. Just to be clear. This equilibrium is consciously striven for. Not luckily stumbled upon by random accident.

With a completely functional operational landscape one's focus becomes strikingly clear: maintain operational homeostasis in order for the flow of life to continue, unobstructed. Systems adhering to this "art of placement" position everything, mentally and physically, where utility can be maximized. Creating an expectationless environment where freedom is encouraged to thrive. And because there's so much variability through context. Continual, contextual re-evaluation is required to maintain current levels of maximum utility; while exploring new areas for advancement.

Organizational sustainability shouldn't be a responsibility of the systems you build. It should be a quality within you, which extends itself to surrounding systems. Systematic viability is not about maintaining your life through detached, overly managed static perfections. Capable of existing only in states of suspended animation. Human systems thinking is about creating structures that allow you the flexibility to adapt (flex, stretch, or contract your universal fabric) to whatever changing circumstances require. Above all, your systems must reinforce the message of your purpose by supporting you at your core. No discrepancies allowed.

Creating systems for yourself is not about removing the joy from living. It's about surrounding yourself with an operational environment, which prepares you to live the best of yourself and elastically adapts to your journey. Best of all, you set the pace of your life through the systems you surround yourself with. Living

5 : Human Systems

at the rate your universal fabric is capable of absorbing makes life much simpler because you control the inputs and the outputs. This permits us enough healthy distraction, by being immersed in the moment, so we don't become overwhelmed with all the things we have to do. Make it a point to understand the flows and techniques best suited to how you work. Putting human systems to work for us requires that we identify, codify, and implement strategies to cultivate smoothly running process flows from raw information streams. Our operational aptitude directly impacts the circulatory health of information streams throughout our universal fabric by coordinating our life's energies.

When making changes to your systems understand how the information you add, remove, or repurpose will affect flow patterns. Repurposing resources must occur until a dynamic homeostasis is achieved in the complete operational picture. Build systems that support you. Those that allow you to experience unobstructed continuity, measured by focus on what is important. Just keep in mind, it is impossible to rely on systems to the point where they will account for a lack of awareness or intuition. In successful systems, balance is a delicate mix of internal and external structures and policy has to be built into design. The flatter a system (the less hierarchical), the easier it will be to create and manage. As an architectural rule of thumb, strive to make your mental and physical environments a reflection of who you are at your core. Doing so will allow you to think and act as an extension of your creation. Build workflows that facilitate only necessary mental and physical connections. Beyond your established flow, experience the eclectic zeal of free-floating semantic connections resulting from the foundational functionality of your life-long investment.

The operational efficacy with which you live will have a profound effect on your quality life and it will affect the outcome of various scenarios you experience in infinite ways. With a complete, operationally mapped environment a flexible method of "everything in its right place" workflow will exist and thrive. Always remember the only systems that matter are the ones that work for you. That life is change is indisputable. The sooner you set yourself up for it, the better off you'll be. Wouldn't you agree?

5.1 : Problem Solving

All fights are won or lost in the stare down. A telling event indicating who commits to the death. I think it is common knowledge we are all a mirror to our problems, but who is winning the stare down? Fears or us?

We need to solve problems blocking our path and assimilate knowledge gained into our universal fabric before moving on to the next trial by fire. You don't have to take your problems everywhere you go, but if you don't solve them you will. Instead become a lockstep smith. Solve one problem before moving on to the next, if you seek to build a solid foundation from which to grow. The sooner you identify current snags and proactively address them, the more rapidly and confidently you'll progress. There are many ways to solve, but it is essential that we address what is pertinent to us completely alone. School is out of session for good. You ready to be the student and the teacher?

Every problem is unique and deserves to be approached as such. The answers of others never bring the same internal fulfillment as your own experience-based conclusions. This has to do with additional understanding you gain by venturing solo, all the way through the problem solving obstacle course. Asking relevant questions and then answering them in daring fashion. If needs be, battling all hell. Solving problems requires living the natural course of an experience and going step-by-step through the learning curve. All the way to the solution. Please, take a few moments to learn the phrase, "I fucked up and I'll fix it". Cause guess what? If you screw anything up along the way, it's your responsibility to... I'm sure you know the rest!

Mistakes are catalysts urging you to reinvent yourself. Learning opportunities that take only milliseconds to make, but sometimes eternity to correct. Learning to live around them may seem like a good short-run "if it ain't broke, don't fix it" workaround; but in the long-run hinders potential in ways unimaginable. Knowing how to navigate roadblocks is never ideal. You can only avoid real problems for so long. In which case the only honorable thing to do is speed up and brace yourself to go through them in order to self-actualize. Welcome to "The Wall". It's not a fun memorial, but many of us have been through it to get what we want. So what are you waiting for? While the thought is fresh rip off bandages hiding failures, heal properly, and move on. It's tough to get back on track, but the obvious correction process is what drills in your head not to error again. Make sure to absorb, lest lessons be wasted on deaf ears. Knowing what works is just as important as knowing what doesn't. And your painfully constructed learning curve must know both (equally) for you to have gained contextual relevance. You first move through, then past; but you never forget. Time to cowboy up. "Yee haw!"

Looking for answers from another is like asking for strategies from an opposing army's general, because only you can solve your problems with your best interests in mind. The issue with not solving on our own is that control mechanisms, put into place to displace reality, end up creating more of a hindrance than an advantage. You have to live problems to solve them and the only way to do this is to jump right in and start swimming through complexity. The unknown marks the

5.1 : Problem Solving

spot. We must have faith and move forward by trusting our intuition, while exploring even unlikely pathways. Like forceful rushing waster seeking exit anyway possible. Often times the only plausible solution is questionable and we are alone with our instincts. Still we must trust that things will be resolved in our favor if we continue on, learning through uncertainty. After all, faith is not seeing the answer; but trusting it is there.

Taking yourself out of the equation is a good first step, which greatly increases the accuracy of efforts. Hell, in some cases this might even solve problems! This means sidelining short-term self-interests to identify long-term, sustainable solutions that satisfy all criteria. Often times we are too close to problems to remain objective. Don't be misled. Distracting symptoms aim to derail. Voyage to the root of causes. Get a good look at what you are dealing with. If you arrive at the core of various other issues that require attention, before you can get to where originally planned, commence at a newly christened beginning. You must root to solidify your solidarity. Why? Because, the lower the roots are the higher the tree grows.

So often it is surprising how multiple issues can all be traced back to the same foundational crevasses. Starting from scratch requires patience at a time when we just want to figure out a solution, quickly as possible to mask the void. Fast is slow and slow is quick. An experienced hand knows this is the time to be patient in the short-run so as to progress rapidly in the long. Even though an immediate advance may seem so magnetic to our resource allocation intuitions, travel the arduous righteous path. A common phenomenon is that problems magically solve themselves when we decide to spend adequate time walking this respectable road with them. Hand in hand. Arm in arm.

Having a singular focus is critical. The fewer variables you alter at once, the more thorough your comprehension to understand cause and effect outcomes of immediate actions. This is especially relevant to the problem solving process because changes only make sense in the context of your control method (your individual approach). Keeping all-other-things-constant (AOTC) is money when searching for variation, positive or negative. It's also helpful to institute return-to-zero capabilities—just in case. Especially when experimenting with transitory information states to tweak parameters this way and that. Until it is determined whether a problem has a solution or has been solved, we have to deal with the manageability of all options so as not to disrupt correctly functioning areas of our lives. Life doesn't stop and start when you want it to. Therefore development is never justified at the expense of forward motion. If you indulge in privileged rest stops you only hurt yourself by disconnecting from the always-spinning gears of reality. Trust me this will stunt future growth opportunities, because you'll never learn how to run and keep pace with what is really happening in the now. Life moves so fast that if you're not careful you'll end up stranded with your dick in your hand. Overall balance is not worth compromising for a solution that is at best minimally valuable, so clean (self-document) as you go.

Visualization helps us consider possibilities and whether it makes sense to use leaps of logic or the historically relied upon default: trial and error. Regardless of the methods we utilize, obvious areas of connection can be beneficial melting pots to generate options. Most judgment errors have to do with us not permitting enough space for intuitions to be explored. If you experience severe gridlock try leveraging the syncretism binding similar previously solved problems within patches of your universal fabric.

Embrace a fresh perspective. Look at a problem from different sides and angles. For the same solution set will rarely be across-the-board applicable. Even the same problem can assume a completely different

5.1 : Problem Solving

idiosyncratic nature when perceived through two sets of eyes. If you encounter resistance ask, "What am I missing?" Take the time to determine what is lacking from your aptitude: knowledge, experience, a skill, etcetera. This is your new focus for the time being. It is up to you to bridge the gap. If you skip this work, done unto yourself is the biggest foundational disservice.

Finding answers to our problems does not mean scouring the earth in search of knowledge aligned with a divine, static perfection that can be tested against the entire universe now and forever. There are no such absolutes. Seeking the firm, imprisoned is the talent evolution has respected in our kind—tends to be the biggest mistake people make. Assuming the end-all, be-all of a solution is within mortals' reach. Ironically the search for these trivialities is often what ends up throwing our world out of sync. This drive for certainty unbalances and reveals that our fears are in fact getting the best of us. At some point considering the next level of efficacy or further refined strategy to solve a problem more perfectly must be scrapped or it will interfere with other actions requiring undivided attention. Don't complicate your life. Keep it simple. On the flipside, if the level of simplicity you are aiming to secure becomes complex and difficult; you have gone to far once again. Remember, simple and easy. Know when to call it a day. When good enough is enough. Embrace solutions that work in the moment and improvise if you must. If answers help you master challenges to the point of non-inhibition, problem solved! You can always optimize a working model that requires fine-tuning down the road.

Be careful not to fall prey or become a slave to the pitfalls of premature optimization. I'm referring to trying to polish a solution so thoroughly and completely that you go far beyond what is necessary and invest way too many resources, well past the point of payoff. Let's say you try to nail down finality, before the time has come to do so. No matter how much forethought you invest, the universe is likely to challenge your solution sometime in the future and you'll need to adjust. For most problems a "good enough" solution does just fine until the next variation comes along. Remember, not all answers have to be ground into details for supreme digestion. Unless you seek a standing ovation for each batch of colossal flatulence produced. For certain answers capturing the "essence" is sufficient. Refinements through use will naturally occur as a result of increased exposure to living our solution. Think "optimization through daily living". Once you have your answer don't waste time. Make a conscious decision to let go of what will become baggage to your next problem solving effort. Just don't treat the problem until "treating it" becomes the problem. Trust your subconscious to retain necessary solution components should you encounter a similar foe in the future. Simplicity is a state of mind. Learn to think it.

The problems we have are the ones we allow ourselves to fixate on. Worrying about what we cannot even attempt to solve makes no sense. Focus on what you can attempt to approach and manage what you have yet to solve, while brainstorming possible solutions. Hint. Quantity not quality. I caution you. Avoid micromanaging and lean toward a broader awareness within the peripheral of your conscious. Tend to your problems as children that demand constant care and once solved require a close eye just in case they become recalcitrant. When you reach your learning curve's summit—solution in hand—integrate newly acquired problem solving tactics into your control method by exercising them until they become trusted components of your nomadic knowledge database. Never lose sight of the fact that we hold the answers to all our problems and therefore our liberation. Seek not temporary escape, but permanent relief from that which you must battle on the quest to understand thyself.

5.1.1 : Focus

Life is full of all too common scenarios for which we'd be rich, had we nickel for each separate incident. Allow me to share one gem I've had the "pleasure" of experiencing time and time again.

"So Carlitos, what do you focus on?"
"I focus on what is important."
"So what's important?" she asked.
"Everything." I replied.

Keep your head out of the game, but your eyes firmly fixated on the prize. To ponder higher purpose, withdrawn from immediate action, is to dilute your transformative power and jeopardize an opportunity to establish the deepest possible connection with the experience at hand. Focus should be reserved for activities that are of the utmost value to your life's mission. For there is a positive correlation between one's ability to concentrate and doing that for which they felt they were made. Sharpening our mind's edge to determine this purpose requires rediscovering passion at this deeper level of understanding for our true focus to emerge and continue gaining momentum.

There are many directions for us to choose from, but none as important as the path we carve for ourselves. Fashioning this meaningful corridor has to do with our ability to buckle down. It translates to maintaining a here and now attention span aimed at accomplishing what is critical and begins with asking the following question. "What is your elemental course of action"? In essence, what's the most important thing you need to do, to move the ball forward in the realm of your life's purpose, immediately. Live this illustration and everything else falls into place. Keep the momentum going by building on a smart decision with another.

Focusing is not the act of limiting what is seen. Rather the decision to choose where we allocate life's resources: time, energy, passion, love, etcetera. Identifying and acknowledging manifestations, residing in peripheral awareness, allows us to come to terms with reality and no longer betaken off course by what once commanded our energy in various frivolous directions. We all want to move forward and find our place in the ever-expanding universe, but such is an impossibility if we do not acknowledge realizations by adapting how we choose to live within our individual circumstances. Your conscious and actions have to believe in the same dream for intended manifestations to materialize.

It's important not to divert from your original intent. Keep your focus razor-sharp so that any distractions are kept at bay. I mean this not only in the immediate sense during action, but also in the broad view. Where our focus has to do with the accumulation of larger macro concentrations of energy to which our life is devoted. Conscript contractive levels of focus to bring you from the wide to the narrow and keep your mindset technical. Look to where you want to go and command the power of one focus. Control your explosion. Be a sniper rifle. One shot, one kill. Not a spray and pray Saturday night special. Where your willpower is dispersed and inaccurate. Assuming it's even functional.

What? Are you afraid you're going to be missing out on something else? Hence the cold feet. Actually, you will be missing out on something very important if you

5.1.1 : Focus

don't focus: getting to know yourself better and ultimately creating a meaningful life in the process. Ah the myth of missing out. I don't buy it for a second. Don't allow yourself to drift upon the sea of life. Directionless and waiting for whatever winds come to fill your sail. Focus on what's important and let insignificant bullshit sink into the abyss. Devote time and energy to that which will keep your soul afloat and protected during life's unpredictable storms.

Focus on exactly what needs to be done by directing your energies toward rewarding outcomes. What you do not need to do, don't. Don't focus on expectant possibilities. If you become emotionally invested in an outcome, you will inevitably restrict its likelihood due to of a lack of focus upon that which would actually contribute to it happening. You know, just like the guy who tries to "get the girl". We all know the badass who ends up conquering her doesn't even give a shit cause he's focused on something else. In the end, you cannot control what happens. All you can do is tweek parameters within your control method. That's it. Examine the process of your current actions because they directly influence. Self-limiting, in appropriate ways, can prove surprisingly effective. Eliminate avenues you already know are dead-end roads leading to camp "Nowhere". Outlaw and murder illusions of grandeur. They undermine giving all attention to the task at hand. Focus on what you can do by practicing the lost art of direct action. Know what you have control over and what you don't so you can work productively and not waste time. In all realty, the opportunity cost of pissing your life away is far more costly to your spirit and to society. Wouldn't you agree?

Focus is less about restriction than it is about enticing ourselves to trust and just believe in the possibility of something greater so we overcome fears in our path. Confronting internal demons has a way of magically crystallizing focus. This in turn causes less desirable, secondary options to lose their appeal. As our manifestations for the greater lead to supreme confidence fueling actions, so does our focus begin to take on a single-mindedness toward accomplishing that which is now shaping itself into destiny. At this juncture, special meditation isn't necessary to achieve concentration. Experiences become so intense that awareness levels automatically reach one hundred percent plus.

What you focus on will determine the results and effectiveness of your focus. What you focus on will eventually lead you to where you are and where you will go. What you focus on is what you will attract into your life and what you will become.

Focus on the process of your journey and let individual moments build on each other. Don't try to prematurely link your journey's steps. Trust that the dots will connect and one day you will know what masterpiece of a life they reveal. Focus on the actions you are deciding on to channel your energies and the quality of inputs you are relying on to fuel your passage. Regardless of whatever mental invasion attempts to steal your focus, walk the course of integrity everyday by holding the line with your life. No matter what. Stop diluting your energy by looking in too many unproductive directions and spreading yourself anorexically, supermodel thin. Be surgically precise and show the world who you are in your purest concentration.

5.1.1.1 : Mindset

Rule your mind's airspace lest you not be able to taxi the runway of possibilities and soar to magnificent heights. Transforming your thoughts begins by defending the boarders that surround your cerebral landscape. Nothing that you possess—materially—is anywhere near as valuable as the psychological ownership of your mind. Regardless of excuses on why your mindset wavers, it is important to remember that nobody (but you) is inside your head. Unless you allow it.

Your mindset is the catalyst through which change is possible because you determine its current state. You create associations necessary for moving forward. By adjusting your outlook life implements a natural process of casting away that, which is no longer you. It is only by guarding and tending this very valuable mental real estate that we garner the strength to confront adversity, when walking in different pairs of shoes. No matter how tempting, don't let anyone—especially you—interrupt your higher thought process. You'll regret it. Keep your mental radar sharp to avoid bullshit and its pontificating pimps.

Establishing the modality of your mind begins with recognizing values and then identifying credible principles, aligned to embrace them tightly. Subsequently, selected principles become guideposts for creating processes that encourage desired behavioral outcomes; through choices in directed living. Once we have identified appropriate processes (those that reinforce desired behaviors), it's time to integrate these independent components into our universal fabric. Along the way making adjustments to avoid compromising our entire life system's homeostasis. With practice various mental architectures emerge out of amassed experience. Based on these atomic constructs we become able to identify the sequential logic behind our mindset's archetype and its virtual construct as an entity.

When your mindset is obsessed with something that is restricting your ascension, everything becomes an extension of that fixation. Nurturing a liberated mindset directly correlates to how freely we formulate the mental associations necessary to transcend human conditions. Any unnecessary associations restrict the most productive use of our mental cache. Control is only necessary to corral your thoughts when you are permitting your mindset to go against who you are. When you reach the core of yourself and live a heightened state of awareness, aligned with a higher purpose, basking in the freedom each moment brings becomes the norm.

A mindset representing our chosen enduring modality (one that we have carefully constructed with respect to the virtues we hold dearest) is the single most valuable construct we can and will ever own. To be automatic—poetic in motion—in one's functioning requires trusting sources of intuition and establishing an attitude supporting the expression of your soul and the emanation of your higher purpose.

5.1.2 : Control Method

Our control method is the applicable skill set through which problems are approached by comparing intricacies to previous foundational successes. Internally coagulating similarities of knowledge acquired through various experiences. A lens constructed and polished over time. The toolbox where diverse mental equipment, certified through previous problem solving endeavors, is stored for future reference. The extent to which our problem solving capabilities thrive depends on how consistently we utilize and refine our methods of control. You don't want to be a one-tooled problem solver. How many well-developed, loaded weapons do you have in your arsenal? Is your game as well-rounded as you think it is?

Think shooting from the hip or relying on Kentucky windage is the key to survival—why? Fear of investing the proper amount of time to do things right? Safety always only comes from developed skill. Alleviate any and all dread through preparation. This is where objective intellectual labor determines standards of approach. Making you think before you act. Perfecting the art of you. Fuck living vicariously through sets of pre-established guidelines. Live through yourself. Competition is about levels of standards applied to oneself.

Demonstrations are unwarranted aftermath. There are those that have to get their "fix" of comparative bullshit to grind out the best of themselves. Hey, whatever it takes to keep you motivated to continue searching for truth. However once it's just you, you will move much faster cause of less proving.

Many things become involuntary with practice, but you must acknowledge that when an action is executed—whether you're aware or not—you are ultimately responsible for where the bullet does or does not land. Regardless if it hits the intended target or causes regrettable collateral damage. This is why it is important that we stay focused and that as the trigger is pulled, we are disciplined and in control of our actions.

Control can be a valuable commodity when directed at areas of life where useful. I am not referring to an acquired state of permanent equilibrium—the goal of many accurately diagnosed control freaks. Such compulsiveness has to do with creating defense mechanisms to counteract reality as a compensation factor masking deeper issues. This is not only unhealthy, but severely retards the expansion of our awareness. Although these people understand the concept of control, they seek to realize it in areas where it is not natural or possible to achieve without causing some type of internal or external corruption. Eventually leading to perversion in one of many forms. Once again confirming that one cannot circumvent their own humanity without repercussion.

Purposeless manipulation is useless, anal behavior. There should be logic-based reasons why control makes sense. Learning how you learn is about perfecting failure. Refining your method of control is about reducing your level of exposure to undesirable outcomes through fine-tuning procedures, in ways other than performance. An activity for those who want to hone a precise knowledge of their own abilities.

5.1.2 : Control Method

Self-limiting directly corresponds to positive enhancement of one's spectral awareness. By pulling focus to notice subtleties, in selected factors, we begin a dissection process to determine what requires attention. Accuracy during this autopsy is critical in identifying root instigators causing what we hope to address. This is why you have to maintain maximum fidelity and test your control method honestly. Living it out exactly as you say it is. Not just when you feel like it, but all the time. Otherwise truth revealed in the awareness of activity goes unnoticed. In the connected moment we find truth and the strength to continue living it. For your own good, stay tuned to your station.

Think back to the constructs to which you were exposed to understand what draws you to your way. From childhood on. Personally, I write like a painter. The endeavor of formulating through the medium of a canvas is highly similar to the verbally aesthetic synergy I apply to language in its written form. Plus, the name you see adorning the work completely created it. Not some additional 30–100 unlisted "helpers" who touch the average, traditionally published book these days. We all have our own unique way of looking at the world. Varied perspectives are necessary because not all points of view are best suited for every situation. With that said, beware of institutions that aim to clone thought processes.

Personal Zen is recognized in the immediacy of life. Not some terrarium like atmosphere with nothing deviating out of place. It's saying what you want to say. Doing what you want to do. Living in a way that is connected to every moment. Through boundaries we implement and are in constant contact with. So as to avoid clogging experiential arteries. Those unable to reach this heightened state may not see it this way, looking in, because they have no nothing to resort to. In this sense our control method is very much a savior during times we require something within our lives to gravitate toward. Keeping our minds out of the gutter and focused on what we can do in spite of less than favorable situations or the powers that be.

Turn not to the philosophies of rotted civilizations. Especially those showcasing methods of analytics that treasure communally established, static detachments over personally deduced estimations. Far too much time is spent defining boundaries for siloed communities, which safe house scientific methods to the point of weakening how individuals actually tune theirs. In the end what matters is what works for you. People who understand this reach new heights. Crashing through vicissitudes never thought possible. Bam! Bam! Bam! One to the next. Just thriving and finding peace in the process. People who can't achieve desired results have to involve ego to prove their place. If you do not follow your own intuition and alter the mistakes, errors, and inconsistencies of your control method; you are just plain stubborn.

There are a lot of things we do not need to know. Those that have no relevance toward what must be done. Basically just snippets of information that we could live without because they do nothing for us. Except waste our thoughts and time. Forget them. What am I referring to? For one, not taking feedback from others. Most likely anything they have to tell you binds with their value system, not yours. If willing to alter yours because of what they tell you, then you have just become a follower of others and not the leader in your life. Show and tell is over. The only person that you need to be telling things to is yourself.

Match the coherence of your inner voice to an a priori agnostic approach. Following external estimations for situations requiring internal participation will simply deadlock us into an emotional holocaust. Creativity is a must when avoiding these unsolvable puzzles. Don't look at results from others. Only look to your tendencies. A result can be misleading as luck can

5.1.2 : Control Method

always influence a twist of fate when you least expect it, and that has no reflective barring on whether you did or didn't do what you had to. With consistent behaviors come results. That and placing yourself in circles other than which you already find yourself. Scary new testing arenas from which you have the most to gain.

Almost all information, including numbers, is in some way skewed. The devil happily resides in details and doesn't plan on moving out anytime soon. That is why we have to become expert practitioners of the parameters by which we interpret and determine. This can only be accomplished if we construct our own guidelines based on self-derived values and with respect to the reality we experience. It all comes down to gathering our own G2 and making our own decisions.

6 : Transcendence

Transcending is not about eliminating the unwanted and controlling everything else. It's about constantly seeking new connections and reconnections with what our deepest sensibilities and soul desire. It's actively breaking free from what holds us back. Not passively waiting for the storms of life to pass. There's always another shit storm on the horizon "thanks" to Mr. Murphy. That's life, get used to it. Transcending is not about "trying" our best. It's about delivering on the goods by actually doing shit to change for the better.

Life is not a fucking democracy for your internal monologue to debate whether you get down to business and get your shit together. In order to function correctly, a democracy requires intellegence that doesn't turn against itself at the worst possible time. Birth your thoughts out in the open and just face the truth. You'll have to do shit you don't want to do in order to get to where you want to go. Plain and simple. So bite the fucking bullet and get on with it. Do what you need to do in spite of limitations. Do what you need to do in spite of shitty circumstances. Do what you need to do to overcome whatever is holding you back from realizing the ultimate you. You don't have to be perfect. You just have to accept reality, decide to change, and move forward. Come to terms with where you are along your journey by looking reality straight in the eyes and don't be naïve by trying to solve your problems by lining them up to the within-reach answers of others. It's unrealistic to think we can arm ourselves with prepackaged knowledge to conquer our unique issues. Trying to secure closure this way will do nothing but frustrate you because, "you" in all reality haven't solved shit. You've just applied a half-ass, quick fix patch to the hole that is your problem and it's not going to hold no matter how much you hope and pray. So many people fallback on shortcuts and that is why they are caught in self-created, viciously cyclonic cycles of ill-fated improvement blitzes. They have not put in the time to do things right. For that they will suffer as a result of shortsighted impatience. So be it. Pain is what they must feel until they have learned to do things the right way. Only something they can realize and decide to modify themselves. Just shut up, accept responsibility, and work to change. Think there's a better way? Let's have it.

Life is simple. There is only reality and your decision to accept and move forward or reject truth and remain stagnant. Teeter-tottering between fears and expectations. If you want to live a lie your whole life, go ahead. The world is waiting for you to do just that. Don't worry because if that is what you choose you'll fit right in with every other non-thinking, non-acting lame-o. To me that sounds much harder than rejoicing in the pure bliss of being yourself, but the choice is ultimately yours. To transcend is to go beyond so we can reach a path that will lead us to inner peace and contentment. In the process of arrival we may have to go through hell countless times. So what? How bad do you want to experience the greatest feeling man can ever know?

During transcendence, everything familiar within an experience—past and present—settles in it's intended place to reveal a peace from connectedness to truth.

6 : Transcendence

What has been, what is, and nothing else. Maintaining an openness to this moment creates the possibility of expounding on that truth and learning more—what is to come. Along the journey of life, experiences encompass different meanings. Precisely why we must have the strength to hold onto that, which binds with our soul regardless of its current expression in the present.

There is never decisiveness accompanying ascension. Only a fleeting peace resulting from an ever-expanding understanding, that is constantly slipping away. This is why we always have to seek reconnection to this transcendence. If achieving a connection were sufficient we would never have to seek it again. Such is a fantasy not worth realizing. Because only through our journey to reconnect are we once again reunited with the life we are here to live and the exhilaration that accompanies living it.

This is a special time when it is wise to pay heed to occurring mental transitions. In hope of familiarizing oneself with a general pathway to find bliss once again. When one internally reconnects, established is a union between the person and the balance that exists for them. An equilibrium that previously could not be perceived because it is impossible to confirm until arrived at. In an instant you feel at home. During these moments one realizes that many things in the past have been impressions of existence and nothing more. Now having experienced transcendence a person understands what is real, true, and that for which no substitute exists. We find what we are looking for in the process of existing as such that requires it.

The strength to transcend comes from reconnecting with who we are and existing as we are, at our core. In this place we find natural assurance to be ourselves. Confidence is restored as we are, once again, reassured in our identity. Here we are able to align the obvious areas of connection in our lives and enjoy what brings us to a purpose in the present.

You will have to sort through way too much bullshit to find even a sliver of what you desire. Always be learning and burning. Look for what is valuable and then have the courage to release what is unnecessary toward your intended purpose and move on regardless of fear or ego. Only by experiencing the transcendence we are capable of reaching, through connectedness to deep meaning, will we be able to risk it all and seek ultimate fulfillment. The more we understand ourselves, the more we begin to embrace the unavoidable futility of what it means to be human. Working with this reality can be a shitty or amazing experience depending on our attitude and how successful we are as cultivators of destiny.

6.1 : Maintaining Solidarity

Consistency equals change. Nothing makes up for time in the saddle. Everyday is a new opportunity to test ourselves by exercising our discipline to do what we need to do. How do you become disciplined? Just like anything else. You practice it daily. Through everything you do. The price we pay to remain on our journey is our commitment to constantly seek to learn more about ourselves. Going to the next level of whatever it is we do. Our journey is an ongoing, self-education process of guarding the newfound sense of who we are and moving forward in a direction that will nurture it. As we find direction, and are reassured in our solidarity, inner strength is affirmed and we can once again test ourselves in close proximity to what would earlier derail us. We owe it to ourselves to stand our ground when it comes to being us. The more we understand who we are, the greater our gathered confidence to be ourselves to the fullest. Regardless of the situations we find ourselves in or the people that surround us. Be yourself from the roots of your core to the extent of everything you touch.

The ordinary becomes extraordinary when you do it. It doesn't take work to see life's truths, but it does take work to live them. Upholding progress requires regular scheduled maintenance. Once you get where you want to be you've got to do the regular work to maintain or you'll simply start regressing. Premature celebrations of results yet to come are the telltale signs of newborn, junior rookies. It is egotistical and naïve to think we can learn something through a single experience and be finished for good. We must constantly reinforce life's lessons through a healthy, daily dose of testing to be reacquainted with the humbling truths they teach. Make sure you get yours. Hold yourself accountable. If you want to be amazing just do what you say you are going to do. Take it down! Be a finisher! Don't talk shit, do shit! This alone will set you apart from those who talk a good game, but can't walk the walk. Everyday ask yourself, "Did I move the ball forward?" If the answer is "No", then get off your ass and do whatever it takes to make it a "Hell yes!" If you start acting like a little bitch and require a gut check, test yourself hard. Until your perspective shifts and you once again appreciate your opportunity to do something great with your life.

In the end, when you are on your deathbed—should you be so lucky to make it that far—the only thing that matters is how you feel about your life in your heart. That's "the" litmus test. Life's real barometer. Whether you can live with the decisions you've made and rest in peace or not. Our conscious is an internal genius. Reminding us exactly what we need to do. What is it telling you to do so you can turn a corner in your life? I know it takes time to navigate life's blue waters, but are you at least on the right track to plotting that course? "How do I know which direction is the right one?" you ask. Easy. The hard one. The one actually worth your precious time? What the hell are you waiting for? An invitation to your own life? Well, here it is. You've been served.

Give your best by serving yourself in a way which serves us all. Stay focused, patient, and humble to make everyday a day for the books to remember.

6.1 : Maintaining Solidarity

History is always in the making. Just depends whether you make it memorable or regrettable. When things get tough remain faithful to who you are. Stick to your guns and always be your own hero. There will be times when no one is on your side. No problem. Teach yourself to love challenge and you'll be fine. I promise. If you decide to experience the harshest reality possible, dragging yourself through hell when you test yourself, nothing that life can throw at you will faze you. Others will be holding on for dear life and to you it will just seem like another day that you tell yourself "It is my job to dig up the will to move forward because I still have to do what I have to do today, regardless." That my friend is the type of attitude I am fucking talking about! Good, bad, sick or sad; it does not matter. If you have to go it alone to protect yourself from people who are tainted in ways which restrict you from realizing the fullest you, so fucking be it. We can't have any of their stupid antics holding us back. Remember, let nothing and no one interfere with your self-actualization. Don't take shit from anybody. Be the rock on which others break their bullshit selves upon, not the other way around.

Mind your business, own your peace. Expect to find nothing but hypocrisy until you look within to match what is in your heart. When your life is focused on what you need to do you will no longer find irritation or distraction from the hypocrisy of humanity. You'll be too focused, transcending through action. A busy life is a happy life. By acting on the things you need to do, stated is your peace. You will find reassurance in your active solidarity because serenity welcomes those who command the winds of change to fill their sail.

6.1.1 : Balance

Prima donnas claim to understand balance. Yet oddly, they have not eliminated inconsistent representations of such associations throughout their universal fabric. As a matter of principle, be hyper vigilant to avoid getting sucked into semantic battles with these eminent "repeaters" of knowledge. Who do nothing more than inform you of shit you do not need to know. This war isn't one that makes sense fighting. For it is without frontline and the unconquerable enemy is time. You are poised to lose big time from the get-go. As demonstrated throughout successful military campaigns, if an opponent has no winnings to offer (intellectual or material) they are not worthy. This principle mistake of engagement is precisely why the sum of life's parts has to be considered as a whole. Otherwise conversations of segmented conquers equate to nothing more than beguiled playground talk. A person only has the fortitude to fight so many wars. Please, choose wisely.

What is balance? Can it be obtained, subdued, or surrendered to in the realm of real? Outside conversations only able to temporarily host the word. I believe so. Of course, not easily. Establishing balance in every moment of life is not always possible when considering lifespan equilibrium. At certain times life's pendulum is in the process of re-centering itself and additional sacrifice temporarily imbalances our whole. Precisely why considering balance in its entirety makes sense. Not just for the individual, but for society in general. For the two are not mutually exclusive, but beyond cross-functionally indispensable.

Physicists study the possible origins of creation by working beyond the sub-atomic level to understand the universe's interrelated expansiveness. My belief is that in each one of our worlds we are a universe. Our re-sounding journey is about understanding ourselves at this same microscopic level. Eventually leading us to consider how we guide efforts in a reactive society. For example. If there is a war going on we are all part of it. Otherwise we are delusional and disconnected from our social responsibilities, acting as reluctant citizens.

Reconsider attractive immediacy in place of wider wisdom. Shortsightedness—a tendency commonly associated with engrained barriers of expression—is a self-imposed, tongue-in-cheek insult because happenings only make sense in the context of entire lived experiences. Reconciling happenings through gun sights leads to foolish cerebrations. Instead, be mature. Surgically accurate in your perception. Link humanity by considering the longview. Many things that initially seem like wasteful trials and tribulations help us connect the dots in ways that would have been unperceivable had we not ditched our narrow, immediate states of interpretation. Instant assimilation is not always possible when attempting to calibrate perspective. The most important thing to remember is that we must keep going, regardless. Continuing to trek in hopes that the next mountain we climb provides a better vantage from which we can establish clarity.

We only truly understand balance to the extent that we familiarize with painful details. Some may refer to this behavior as "over analytical". Me, "unprecedented applied theory". What it means to be well-adjusted, in

6.1.1 : Balance

every sense. Versatile and at home everywhere. An ambassador representative of the behaviors evolution has painstakingly selected as worthy. So why are we self-programming to think otherwise? Because, recorded human history embeds itself through the execution of the natural. Relying on subjectified ego swell. This is why unsung heroes are so important to a society that is coming apart at the seams. They are the patches sealing exposed and dangerous vulnerabilities that society couldn't remain intact without addressing. This is why I encourage becoming one. Before it's too late.

Compartmentalization may numb the pain, but what will permanently heal the wound that is destabilizing your life? Entirety! It's the game changer. Requiring cultivation of enriching curiosity and vigor. Proficient balance resembles an ambidextrous chess match between the mental and physical realms. As no two aspects of ourselves are separable. Whether our physicality or mentality, all of your universe's "parts" are completely modular and interchangeable when it comes to expanding an ever-lasting flow. It isn't necessary for one to pause and halt development. Instead try switching between actionable options. If one part of your life is stagnant, by all means keep trying to unrestrict; but don't neglect other areas you should be living. Most likely something relevant that has been neglected is the holdup. Do what you can instead of adding insult to injury. Alternate. You can't win any personal wars if you lack the ability to be running and gunning. From one obstacle to the next. Pick what your state of mind is prepared for and then go a bit further. Always push boundaries if you hope to get anywhere. And remember, regardless of your current state of existence; you can always do something to enrich your life in a way that compliments you throughout.

Societal equilibrium cannot rely on mass scale collaborations if the individuals involved are not coherently balanced in their own right. This discrepancy will inevitably lead to a caving from within these constructs, which may at first appear satisfactory; but over time reveal the cracks of the members who formed them. Exactly why diversity of unique contributions, balanced through and through, is critical to our survival.

We don't need another chartist, laser pointing a curve or line graph; distinctly rewarded, from what at an ethereal level people like myself are direct proof of. Telling us about some unconnected, distant association that some how makes sense to them and oddly that is why they have to justify it to us. We need widespread truth exemplified through you. Representative of balance applicable in the widest encompassing sense possible. All the way down to the narrowest examples within ourselves. Not ignorant philosophies relying on the chickenshit cover of segmented comparison to sustain terrarium like atmospheres that are doomed to collapse from the get go. Catch my drift? Then show me your balance and I'll show you mine.

6.2 : Your Beginning

Finding one's home through self-exploration fills the heart with unparalleled riches. Fortunately, there are always unfamiliar areas of ourselves; which is why the journey never ends. Discovery is an ever-changing puzzle.

Contentedness comes from living in a way that truth continues to reveal itself to us. Reaching the path of consciousness where we begin to discover who we are and why we are here is a sacred milestone. No matter where or when we come into our own. Confidence builds from trusting oneself and continuing this journey of expansion. To a place where all things meet and you find you. That's really the beginning!

I set out on this journey to understand myself because I have hope. In you, in me, and in the potential of our combined powers. Somewhere buried deep within our subconscious I think we all aspire to leave things better than we find them. Being human we take so much out of the world. My question to you, "So what are you going to give back as a result of your journey?" The crime of it all? Imagine what you would be giving back—right now—if you could overcome your challenges and get to the core of why your heart really ticks.

Here's to you, where your life leads you, and to realizing the dream that you will maximize your potentialities and affirm why you were born. Who knows, maybe you'll even give the rest of us a little something back to give us hope along our journey. That would be nice. Plus I think you owe it to the rest of us unsung heroes. Who sacrifice everything and more just to have something to share with you. It's hard to understand if just starting out, but the experience I'm hoping you seek out is well worth it.

When you are finished reading this book and deem the time has come, I encourage you to burn it and from the ashes realize that everything you need to go on your journey is in your heart and always has been. I'm confident you'll figure out the rest. Fair winds and following seas, my friend. Bon voyage!

Epilogue

So what's the root of our issue? Our god complex is but a single leaf on a tree with many far-reaching roots, extending into the debatable. As a country we've always proudly tethered to an imperialistic identity. Probably why it'd be comforting to arrive at a commonly accepted, simple answer. For instance: the 19th century doctrine of Manifest Destiny, forged through an arduous history of imperialistic worship, is the culprit. However, that's just not the case. Let's be honest. Our behaviors go back further than the obvious constituents of colonization. They are rooted in the essence of life itself. The kill or be killed base trait—opportunism—pounded into every organism's survival mechanism by way of discriminating evolution. It all goes back to who we are—nature.

Although fixating on the future is enticing, we have to look back before we can move forward. All the way back to the beginning. Question the cradle of man and what has brought him a more than fairly deserved share of cultural malaise. What initially delivered humans into the present now presents a conflict of interest. Too much of a good thing has turned us against each other and ourselves. As sapient beings are we not at the helm of our world? So why don't we act like it? Nature provides useful clues in understanding this puzzle, that as a species, we have yet to solve. Let's look back at the pre-diagnostic times of our evolution. Before our egos decided they were no longer obligated to respect natural forces.

Human history is alarming in terms of what it reveals. Ignorance breeds ignorance. Strength breeds strength. Weakness breeds weakness. On and on and on. It would seem destitute to assume otherwise, however. Altering socially engrained behavioral cycles, although difficult, can be accomplished. Don't believe me? Did you know that it's possible to selectively breed behaviors into or out of various animals after only a few generations' time? Humans have a much shorter gestation period. Endless cycles of change can occur within our lifespan. Such is the nature of genius that represents variation and leads to advantage or disadvantage. Contributing to the plethora of traits that will either be selected for survival or segregated for extinction. This begs a question. Are we in complete alignment with behaviors we are selecting to represent us?

Our fatal blind spot? We don't completely comprehend what we are dealing with and for a very good reason. It's almost impossible to see the forrest for the trees when you are a tree. Had humans been tasked with predicting which humanoid ancestor would prevail, from various lineages of what became formally known as "man", we would have been dead wrong. What makes us believe we can choose wisely while dwarfed by impending catastrophes and in the face of so much more adversity, before each conquers thy puny self? I see only one way out. A single chance at salvation by overcoming the human conditions we have been dealing with for centuries.

People must be encouraged to follow the virtues of their spirit. Every unique contribution is a genius variation that time has yet to determine whether it will enable the transcension of our species or not. Individuals

Epilogue

positively developing their areas of confidence stand to impact themselves, society, the planet, all life, and the universe beyond. We just don't know what potentialities exist until we uncover them within ourselves. Not just to each his own, but to all each of our singularly special treasures. The greatest gifts to humanity have the possibility of residing in multiple forms of life: men, women, children, and nature. Personally, I believe they exist in all. Sadly human opportunism expressed as innovation, while grand on many levels, has just helped us work around issues that in all reality are still clouting potential at our core. Helping us circumvent evolution's rules while in return delivering a windfall of demise. Negative tradeoffs as a result of poor choices.

So what does this mean in terms of a suitable prognosis for America's future, based on its kitchen-sink past? Historic plausible deniability has blinded generation after generation. The most recent disconnect—the beginning of the end—was after the Second World War. WWII required the unification of labor systems during a time plagued with doubt as to the world's fate. America came so close to defeat that by the end of the conflict her operational pace, from a production and mobilization standpoint, was unprecedented. This is huge considering this epoch in history is hot on the heels of the Industrial Revolution. Firing on all cylinders had become the norm. No question as to whether we were a powerhouse. Massive momentum, combined with the competitive-cooperative efforts of foreign nations, recharged a "freedom-spreading" rebirth. The US had made it through a hellish windmill semi-intact. In contrast, outside native soil, the industrialized world lay in ruins. A multitude of international commerce hubs, providing livelihood to our foreign brothers and defeated enemies, had been annihilated.

A sweat-stained veil of turmoil was lifted from the American heart. What better a way to mark the occasion than with a new vision for a country of tomorrow.

Bam! The American Dream was born. And it was a heavy, big, and hungry monster of a mouth. Yet our economics could feed it. Why worry? Enjoy! No end in sight. Demand was high and America was supply. We were "the" brand to buy. We had it good. No competition, therefore no standards. Instead of cultivating intellect and ingenuity we did everything easy way. We compensated with size. Bigger cars, bigger houses, bigger dreams, bigger stars, bigger food, bigger fucking everything. Meanwhile, those in the recovering world (allies and enemies alike) were forced to start from scratch. The restoration of Europe revealed more than its people's resilience. It showed that ideologies abroad had shifted. At a time when the recovering world was surviving on a steady diet of humble pie, we encouraged our ego to "think big". What we didn't see is that this would catch-up and haunt us in the decades to come.

The self-prophesied values defended by the baby-boomers mark the birth of the ego surge now referred to as the American Dream. Ignorance at its finest. Paramount proof of how confidence can be confused with culturally misguided behavior. The ideologies of this generation are completely reality agnostic. Overall, boomers enjoyed—and continue to—uncapped and undeserved opportunity and prosperity. Beyond any society's wildest imagination—during anytime in history! This is why the rest of the world has always had a fascination with the American Dream. But that's all it is. A dream, not reality. Boomers are synonymous with the cushiest existence in the history of man. They've milked advantages to the point that nothing is left. Unless you we're part of this eminent domain movement you've been disenfranchised aka fucked big time.

Fast-forward to today. Life has become ugly competitive. As a result, we witness the "Dream" crumbling everywhere. What happened is that while the US was affixing the words "La-La Land" to its marquee the rest of the world became resourceful. Creative through necessity. Far better with a whole lot less. All the while pressured to deliver. The American lifestyle dealt them this fate. Through almighty and powerful, overtly proud unjustified ignorance. This trait has not died in us, but man are we a different country.

One can't help but notice our disparaging, rotted social climate. America's founding ideologies have been backseat raped by politically inclined monsters seeking total control in the name of democracy. Today Americans don't even own their home soil. Corporations do. Most of them globalized or foreign to maintain a competitive edge at the expense of disguised, non-localized dwindling morality. And for what? Well for one thing, it costs to live the "Dream". Those who aspire to must cut corners and leverage to the hilt. And I'm not just talking money. I'm talking ethics, standards, health, and any other realm in which we are negatively affected as a result of indulgent behavior gone awry.

Amongst the international super-rich jet-setters—earners through raping our sensibilities—it's common knowledge that the American Dream is only real for them. That is why they don't mind occasionally feeding hopefuls that lack. Who can blame them? They like the hand they are holding. Holy shit they must! They've been holding it for a long fucking time and will continue to squeeze the life out of the back-broken middleclass to maintain power. They'll never relinquish advantages secured through selling their morality downriver because that's all they have left. This is precisely why the "Dream" is a nightmare we won't wakeup from for a long, longtime. The wealthy understand what normal folks seek isn't available, but they sure as hell don't mind trading ethics and clearance selling integrity to us to keep us occupied with illusions of grandeur at our expense. I mean look at modern marketers. Selling us an image of whom we should want to be and in the process making the individual and society as a whole worse off. Goddamn fucking lying criminals with no fucking souls is all they are. Considering the value created throughout our history's past—settlers forward—it's disgusting to see what "the land of opportunity" has become. Today it's hard to find anything of value stamped "USA". The only thing we still manufacture domestically (and to no end) are lies telling ourselves that the American Dream is possible as a reality for everyone. I'm doubtful we will ever acknowledge otherwise because these are fundamentalist behaviors that a narrow-minded history has carved into our heads. If we want to move forward with dignity we have to accept that we've lied to ourselves. That's right. We are to blame.

Today everything is about world markets and connectivity. Sleek technology and the next fucking gadget. Technological advancements have consequentially become confused with classic self-actualization techniques. Modern tools have surpassed human computational abilities. We can communicate faster than we can even process. The limitation in the loop has become our Neolithic behavioral systems. It's obvious. Further technological reliance seems like the only way out, however. Another exists. Did you know, it's still possible to have a life without living on the bleeding edge? Even though corporations don't want you to believe it, technology is not the instant messiah for solving problems that people need to take ownership of themselves. This is why we are so damn lost.

Being an American used to mean something. Today we are just a fat, lazy, and backwards country still holding onto a past that should have never had its place in history. Granted technology has allowed us to grow, but with that expansion we have tugged along our unsolved ills. Converting them into a digital sickness. And gladly spreading this socially transmutable pandemic that has infected the globe. Still, we remain proud of our purpose. Which is what? To connect the

Epilogue

entire world and then sift through a soupy crisis? At that level of complexity it makes me wonder why we think we could succeed then, if we can't now. So where do we go from here?

The real issue lies in transferring relevant knowledge between a change-challenged, pedantic mature generation to one born in an information complexity vortex with their heads up their ass. This proverbial changing of the "lard" can only be accomplished if we sort through humanity's information repositories and shed that which is no longer of value, in fact dangerously toxic. Far too much energy is wasted preserving ego monuments or trying to understand what has little — if any — relevance to our moment. History repeats itself, one way or another, and I for one have seen as many cycles of demented repetition I can handle. Let's change things right now by vowing never to worship or spend another second thinking about the inconsequential. I'll be the first to denounce textbook myths only viable in naïve imaginations. Then I need your help in identifying living treasures who maintain an air of integrity. Real life veterans poised to help younger benefactors identify wisdom and virtuosity. Truly accredited unsung heroes on a mission of utmost importance. Specifically selected because their credibility is born of firsthand experience today and everyday they live and breathe. Can't find any? Then I guess we both know what role you have to fill. Welcome to your new home!

History is full of spoiled brats and bullshit stories. Who knows what really happened? Who cares? I want you to think about what is happening right now. So often what we remember is pounded into our fucking heads by people that want us to remember their shit. Duh! Otherwise we wouldn't. Advice that you shouldn't take unless you have a pound of salt handy. Be skeptical of those synonymous with advantage-laden contexts. Hint, most of the baby boomers. What the fuck happened to them? I'll tell you. Advantage robbed them of what needed to be earned. Looking back it's obvious. Distinctive behavior patterns established at the outset of "Boomdom" could never amount to a cultural character worthy of respect. Nor did they. The responsibility to save the future is in each and every hand. How will we pass Lady Liberty's torch without extinguishing the freedoms her flames protect? Unique contributions from everyone. No exceptions.

In the egotistical race for profits, corporations have revealed three things. They understand necessary business components to creatively innovate and continue reaching new levels of success. Second, the overwhelming technical challenges that continue to present themselves in the face of constant and expectant innovation can be overcome—for now. Ignorance lies in the third. The human component. At the end of the day, everything is about people. The most valuable assets walk out of corporation's doors and into their own lives at the end of each day. Only to return and willing slave once again, if lucky. Even worse are those whose identities are inseparable from a paycheck and whose sad lives consist of "working moments" throw into every pocket of time. Although they may not admit it, the societal backlash is evident. Whatever people's deal with the devil I think individuals have so much more to offer. And this is why, ironically, unencouraged people remain the most neglected area of possibility. They are unmined treasure troves where positive potential value can be excavated, if done sincerely and for the right reasons. A large part of the problem has to do with a lack of enforcement when it comes to the governing ethics in corporate landscapes that overwhelmingly value increased market share, double-digit growth, and quarterly profits at the expense of humanization. Entities acting under such a ruse are in fact ponzi schemes because their devastating exploits leave nothing for future generations that are paying forward with their hopes and lives. What do we get in return?

Epilogue

Condemned to social mazes we have no possibility of avoiding? Gee "thanks!" This is very revealing. Not only of the vicious, self-invoked cycles our economy regularly experiences. Such is powerful macro-proof of micro-challenges we each are faced with overcoming as individuals. We cannot look outside of ourselves no matter how tempting our proficiency in the external. Doing so will ensure collective social ills remain ignored. Suffered through the veins of society's lifeblood. This need not be the case, but it will be if people expect to find themselves in the lost and found of an out-of-control—kill or be killed—industrial complex.

No matter how "positively" marketing departments display their power of persuasion, to influence your opinions, large multinational corporations are not sympathetic to human needs. They are death machines sneeking control. We give our lives. We kill for them. And then when we ask for something in return everything becomes an impossibility. It's such a fucking hypocrisy. They breed certain behaviors into us so we go out and break our fucking backs for them. But be warned! They don't want to see those same sets of behaviors turned toward them. They expect us to be good little bitches capable of ignoring, at an interest's notice, the essence of our germination. Sorry, but that is not how engrained instincts naturally express themselves. Just as in nature you cannot switch genetics on and off to suit your agenda—instantaneously—without disrupting the functionality of a "tuned" organism. Especially traits that have no merit. Even though we can change our psychological patterns, it takes time. And this is exactly why we feel the reprise of negative, self-created social conditions. Companies' collective interests dilute individuals' incentive to follow moral codes and the benefits such brings. Never giving them the chance, then sidelining them if they dare. Don't act like you're married to a corporation that is only dating you. A cheap bastard going Dutch for that matter. They will replace you with a "Yes!" clone in two seconds flat when it suits them. Regardless of the quantity of life you have given the or what they have promised.

Oh how I do "love" corporate communications. Companies claim to have no reserves. Then magically, when disastrous commercial conditions affect their competitors, they fortify by firing people and adding assets to an already swollen portfolio. All bullshit lies formulated at securing the future of a few control freaks at the expense of many individuals with a more humanistically inclined agenda. Money earned in the pursuit of such is dirty because interests to acquire it are guided by self-serving ideals instead of a dedication to help people overcome human conditions and rise above the mundane. I'm not opposed to capitalism, but as long as the evil profit maximization engine is fueled by cloaked values; we are looking at a potentially lethal situation. Our focus needs to be social business. With the primary objective of benefiting society by putting the welfare of people first. Delivering products and services from the heart with the intended gift of humanizing in the realm of good, honest business. Otherwise our identity as people and as a country is in jeopardy of being lost forever. Will we finish strong or even at all? You tell me. How do you make your dollars and where do you spend them?

So you don't like the way things are? I get it. I understand. Where to go from here? Hmmm? The reality is that the status quo will continue because of "me" oriented star cultures that just keep virally replicating. Modern communication environments are the perfect petri dishes for social viruses. With the infected encouraged to seek attention, proclaiming "Look at me! Look at how good I am!" So what if you are good? It doesn't matter if you or I are superhuman. It's easy to just focus on ourselves and proclaim our exception. To only live in our little world. That's why so many do it. If you are so great, then why can't you help solve the

Epilogue

problems within the bigger picture? Starting with you. I guess all that greatness is some how wasted supporting your ego to do otherwise. Oh no? Well then what's your excuse? Go ahead take your time. I'll wait. This will allow me to get some earplugs because excuses are something I don't care to give or hear.

The bulk of humanity lives within the confines of the bell-shape curve. Humanization requires impacting this ninety-nine percent in the middle. The reason it makes sense to focus our energies on empowering the majority is that the combined impact of a few really proficient teacher's pets is miniscule in comparison to a significant portion of the population slightly adjusting their lives. Extensive change by a few, although admirable and appreciated, is simply not sufficient to make up for an entire heel-dragging populous. This is why it's absolutely critical that we all embark on our own journey to in turn transcend the specific human conditions affecting collective progress. This is the only way we can return to society a unique contribution that has been stamped out of testing our limits and leveraging the resulting growth—intellectual and physical horsepower—as knowledge to be shared through action. Eventually culminating in hypocrisy-free products and services. Education equals adoption, and this is exactly what unique contributions are all about. Put on your meta, lateral thinking caps and mine the caves of hidden potential for gems of truth that every human is capable of discovering. We are living during a time when anything is possible and possibilities are endless. So dig until you hit gold, oil, or whatever the fuck is in your soul.

The time has come for America to get her cultural mind out of the gutter. We don't need fresh blood to solve this one. The writing is on the wall. Our idealism is fueling wars, creating problems, and resulting in issues that cannot be offset with overly publicized, band-aid propaganda fixes. If we do not take responsibility for our actions humanity is doomed to repeat its sad history and this is tragic because we are living during a time where this need not be the case. If our unique contributions are aimed at humanizing the world, at the fundamental level of basic human rights, slowly eliminated will be the delta between those who are truly oppressed and the advantages that we must sacrifice to create this bridge. Then we can all start together from the same place. United. This is my vision, this is my dream. Don't worry if you don't know what yours is. That's what your journey will answer.

Even though behaviors are the engine of evolution, our survival was made possible by emotional intelligence. We already started to transcend limiting conditions long ago. Now we just need to have the decency to extend the courtesy to the rest of life we share our existence with. We owe restoration to what we have exploited to get here. We've been able to get ahead of the evolutionary learning curve and can see exactly what we need to do. We need no longer be steered by blind opportunistic instinct. We can breed behaviors and have been for a longtime. Just not with the conscious awareness at our disposal today. We have the capability to transcend the fate of disastrous evolution simply through individual and then collective social change. What got us here isn't what's going to move us forward in a positive direction. We are tasked with evolving to the next version of human. If we refuse we face inevitable extinction, sooner rather than later. Do your part by avoiding the pitfalls of being born within the constraints of societal ignorance. Help me write the next chapter of our history in a tone that future generations looking back, as we are now, will not have the same lingering bad taste in their mouths as we do.

We can do some pretty amazing things when we commit. So let's salvage our noble, endearing roots and transplant them in fertile minds to get back to what will make us proud to be human and proud to be

Epilogue

American. Instead of fixating our energies on what separates, let's put bullshit aside and focus on what unites. The temple of the American spirit has always existed in the heart of its people. That's why we love adventure and those who embrace it. Even though the state of our miasmatic stench permeates everything, it's important to remember that this country wasn't always a place that created strategies to segment the poor amongst poor in a race for self. "US" used to denote "United States". Now it just refers to all we really care about—"us". Ironic, but not really. We weren't always a country that focused on selling product-sets, based on nepotistic values, to every social segmentation under the sun. We are a resilient and determined people who want to see their joie de vivre thrive in the hearts of future generations. Let us look to thought processes throughout history, condemning those that lead down self-destructive paths, by embracing what makes us respect freedom. Not as a concept, but as a reality.

The object of fascination known as the American Dream needs to be annihilated. Silenced for good. Such a utopia is unattainable, unsustainable, and impossible to balance as a culture, as a society, and as a race considered in its entirety. Let this be the end of an infatuation with a lifestyle that never was. It is time for us to in fact define, and own, our evolutionary next step. Let this be the beginning of an era marked by each individual becoming proficient with the lifestyle informatics of their existence. Help me in welcoming the dawn of (your name here)ics. I want you to become a rebel of fashion. To honor your freedom. To voice your opinion through action. If you do not agree with the sign of the times decide to go against the grain. Let your ideas engulf each other and take on a life of their own, till you have a dream. Then set out to accomplish that dream and make it a reality. Like a word, that runs into a song, that turns into an album, that grows into a symphony. The world is a great place, but will not remain so if we abuse it in lieu of solving our problems. Granted there will be more cultural explosions that present addition opportunities to pursue selfish expansion. New outlets to continue overfeeding an already unsurpassed historical ego. When these "opportunities" come around why don't we try something new and get closer to who we really are in the process?

Don't be an evolutionary dead-end. Or you won't make it through the bottleneck every individual must pay penance to pass through. We all have the capability to change multidirectionally. Human evolution tested us and that is why we are here today. Variability was the catalyst fueling our survival. That's why we are adapted to constant change and need to openly embrace it to continue our cause.

I refuse to believe—after pulling myself through a journey of this fucking magnitude—that those whose basic human rights aren't being denied can't change or test themselves at least a little bit for the benefit of all. And that's the sad truth. We are all affected. In all reality, I can't transcend if you don't. None of us can. Humanization's cause will die unless we unite. Unless we fuse our efforts together at the level of sustenant values. If we don't pull ourselves together we are just dwindling embers in the far corners of a barely sustainable fire. Not a powerful united flame. Thank you for taking the time to read my book. I now consider us brothers and sisters in arms.

Pedagogy

Nothing rewards my efforts more than hearing from real people, living real lives. Spontaneous and informal pedagogies chartered not around status or money, but upon the experience and integrity of participants' conscious experience. Come share in an environment that genuinely encourages collision of thought. For touring information visit www.carlitosics.com. I always hope to put a handshake to my readers. Come join me and say "hello!"

www.ingramcontent.com/pod-product-compliance
Lightning Source LLC
Chambersburg PA
CBHW050904160426
43194CB00011B/2288